MW00427370

Perfectly Normal

An immigrant's story of making it in America

Michelle Kuei, PharmD., CPC, ELI-MP

To my dad who taught me discipline,
To my mMom who taught me
strength and determination,
To my brother who taught me compassion,
To my sister who taught me love,
To Joseph who taught me how to live this new life,

And

To all the friends I have encountered on
this journey who taught me who I am.
You are both my teachers and my students.

Introduction

"If you're going to try, go all the way. Otherwise, don't even start. This could mean losing girlfriends, wives, relatives, and maybe even your mind. It could mean not eating for three or four days. It could mean freezing on a park bench. It could mean jail. It could mean derision. It could mean mockery—isolation. Isolation is the gift. All the others are a test of your endurance, of how much you really want to do it. And, you'll do it, despite rejection and the worst odds. And it will be better than anything else you can imagine. If you're going to try, go all the way. There is no other feeling like that. You will be alone with the gods, and the nights will flame with fire. You will ride life straight to perfect laughter. It's the only good fight there is."

—Charles Bukowski, *Factotum*

Years ago, I thought about writing a book. The idea scared me, but it was rattling around in my head for a very long time and like a blade of grass doggedly pushing through the cracks in a concrete sidewalk, it persisted. I wasn't sure what to write about, and second, what if I didn't have anything interesting to say? Lastly, what if the book turned out to be another one of those wannabe best sellers lining the market bookshelves? Days passed in the blink of an eye and I had accomplished nothing, my thoughts busy and afraid. The dream of being recognized as a published author seemed to be so far away from my reality.

When we are afraid, we show up to the world in ways that keep us from fulfilling our potential. Fear keeps us playing small. The most common way we do this is through avoidance. We avoid taking risks, avoid taking leaps, and avoid confronting people because we are afraid of creating conflict. We are afraid of voicing our opinions because we are afraid of being isolated or being judged. We hide in our caves and avoid being vulnerable.

Some of these behaviors are more apparent than others. For example, you might have wondered what it would be like to stand on top of the Statue of Liberty while looking down over the Hudson River, but you avoid heights. You might be afraid of insects, so you avoid that visit to the Amazon rainforest where nocturnal insect tours are a popular excursion. Or you might be afraid of opening up to people, and therefore you avoid all social networking events.

The truth is when we are afraid, we are just not using our true potential and stepping into our superpower.

In April 2018, I enrolled myself in a coaching training program after nearly 20 years working in both retail and hospital pharmacies. What inspired the whole process goes back to my life experiences in early childhood. Those experiences lead me to re-examine every aspect of my own life. Like many people finding themselves at a crossroads, I asked myself these questions: What brought me here today? Exactly what did I have to experience in order to achieve my current state of consciousness? What is my purpose? Why was I born? How can I make a difference? What do I have to offer?

As I began to explore all these deep and meaningful life questions, I thought about writing this unwritten book of mine again. But this time, instead of wondering what to write about and fearing imposter syndrome, I thought, why not just write about myself? Why not share with the world the many inner thoughts that I was never able to reveal before?

I believe that, in a way, we are all our own unwritten books. As human beings, we share so many of the same lived experiences. These bind us together and underscore our interconnectedness. Our souls, our ideas, and our beliefs are linked like a massive tangled fishing net. Your life struggles are just as real as mine, and your challenges in life are just as big as the person's sitting next to you on the subway. Each page we turn leads to a new story in every chapter of our lives.

And there it was: the idea of writing a book, standing right in front of me as I began to expand my own seminar and coaching company in this new chapter of *my* life, but what's different now is that it doesn't look so scary anymore. Every piece of me matters deeply to me. Every story that I share in these pages comes from the bottom of my heart. The struggles, the tears, the desperation, the resilience, courage, inspiration, and the triumph, all the bits and pieces make me the person I am today.

This is not a story wherein the hero—me— saves the world at the end of days. Nor is it a story about a major celebrity who was paralyzed after a car accident and went on to become a spokesperson for a globally recognized organization. This is also not the story of an ugly duckling turned into a beautiful swan. This is a story about an ordinary girl—just like you, your sister, your neighbor, your mother, or someone else in your life—who transformed her life to serve a greater purpose.

I don't need to be a best-selling author on Amazon, nor do I crave the spotlight or fame; this is simply the story of a life lived with courage, love, and vulnerability, written by an ordinary woman who loves many, laughs hard, and lives her life to the fullest every minute. This is a story about seeing the light when everything else is dark.

Chapter

One

"I have learned that if you must leave a place that you have lived in and loved and where all your yesteryears are buried deep, leave it any way except a slow way, leave it the fastest way you can. Never turn back and never believe that an hour you remember is a better hour because it is dead. Passed years seem safe ones, vanquished ones, while the future lives in a cloud, formidable from a distance."

— Beryl Markham, *West with the Night*

I was born in Taiwan, in a suburban town in the northern part of the island. My family lived in a small veteran village—a community sometimes called a "dependent's village" comprised of war veterans and their families—together with my two married uncles, their wives, and their children. The original purpose of these villages was to serve as provisional housing for nationalist soldiers and their dependents retreated with the Kuomintang (KMT) government from mainland China to Taiwan. These villages ended up becoming permanent settlements, forming distinct cultures as enclaves of mainland Chinese in Taiwanese cities.

Most houses were built in the 1950s with straw roofs and mud-and-bamboo walls, and in the 1960s, some were reconstructed with sturdier bricks. The dependent's villages generally comprised anywhere from 10 to hundreds of housing units segregated from the rest of the community, and most of them suffered from outdated facilities and overcrowding. My family shared a 1700-square-foot lot with our relatives, and my family's actual living space was about 800 square feet, roughly the size of an average suburban American garage made of brick.

I was born in this tiny home, the second child of Sue, my mother, and Alan my father. I have a brother, Mike, who was also born here, three years before me. Being the first-born male, Mike received quite a lot of my grandparents' love and care. We lived in this little house until I turned four.

I've always liked old houses with floorboards that creak when you walk across them like ours did. Our village house had an attic on the second floor where I could lie down on a hot summer's day listening to the cicadas singing outside in the trees, and the clock ticking on the wall as I watched the time pass. I find the smell of these old houses-where memories, good and bad, are kept alive-comforting and familiar.

I imagined my life in this house many times; what it would have been like to stay in that tiny space with my uncles, their wives, and all of my cousins throughout my childhood. I would have probably attended school with my cousins. My grandparents would have probably spent more of their time with me and spoiled me with everything I ever asked for, buying me candies and giving me money. Maybe I would have gotten married to someone from the village, because that's what people do here; they marry the people they grew up with. I think that's what my mom and my dad would have wanted for me. I might have developed with a different set of values and beliefs, or have a different outlook on life, and I might have even had a completely different outcome of my own life.

Imagine holding in your hands two cups filled with water you scooped out of the ocean. What each cup holds is essentially the same water, just in two different cups. When you pour the water back into the ocean, it becomes part of the greater body of water again. I imagine myself like that sometimes, being part of an ocean that everyone else belongs to, too. The only difference between me and the person standing beside me are the experiences we have in our individual bodies.

Life is the ocean and we are the waves, being

pushed forward and crashing against the harsh terrain, storming through the roaring sea, and slamming into rocky shores. But no matter where we come from or what struggles and challenges we endure, we are still part of the ocean, the bigger scheme of life.

My parents taught me what it means to overcome your own struggles in life. It all begins with an idea: making the best out of what we have. The reason we left that little house was because my mom, the bravest woman of all time, had a vision of what it means to have a better life. My mom, Sue, is a very strong woman. While we were living with all my relatives, she wasn't entirely happy sharing such close quarters. My oldest uncle and his wife appeared to have gotten the bigger share from the family with more living space at the village house. My other uncle tended to be more assertive and also received more space than my family did. This left my dad, Alan—who is more soft-spoken and much more giving—having very little in the family. Our quarters were cramped and there were sometimes skirmishes among our family members.

"One day, your brother Mike, and cousin, Grace, got into a fight." Mom said. "Mike took a big bite out of Grace, right there on her nose."

"Did you not feed Mike?" I asked. "And of all places, how the hell did he decide it was going to be the nose?"

I laughed so hard every time she shared this story. It was not uncommon for children to fight, but the way my mom described it was very comical. There

4

were other things Mom shared with us throughout the years, like how she had to do laundry for the entire family when she and Dad first got married, and how my grandmother was not very helpful at all in making peace among all these in-laws living together at the house.

When Grandpa found out Mom wanted to move out so we could live on our own, Grandpa didn't speak to my dad for the entire month. But Mom was adamant about moving away from this big family because she had enough of living in 800 square feet with her husband and two small children. She had a vision of what a better life would look like and she was determined to make it her reality. She wanted space of her own, and fought with my dad to take out a mortgage.

It took my parents four years to save up enough money and apply for new positions with higher salaries, and by the time I was four years old, we moved out of the little house of ours and into a bigger and better place—a rental at first—to call home.

The rental house was north of my grandparents' home—an hour to two by car, train, or bus—in an area where there were more rice fields than buildings. Our village consisted of no more than 200 people, and everyone seemed to know everyone. The house was situated below the flight path of a nearby airport, and we used to play outside and watch the airplanes fly overhead during landings and takeoffs. My dad had a job at the local school and my mom got some sewing work from the local garment factory.

Memories from that period in our lives are vivid. One stormy night while dad was away on a trip and it was just my mom, my brother, and me at home, there was a flood. It was night, and rain pummeled our house, quickly filling up our living room with water, turning it into a swimming pool. The power had just gone out and mom lit candles. Mike and I watched with excitement as pots and pans floated by, buoyed by nearly two feet of water that filled every room in the house. Mom put me up on a table at the front of the living room along with Mike. Our front door was open, and we sat, mesmerized, watching the airplanes flying by on this stormy night. I watched one of my dad's big shoes float around in the house like a lonely boat sailing around finding a dock to park. We had quite a few days and nights like this during the typhoon season. Eventually, Dad made a wooden barrier that he would slide into the front door to prevent water from pouring into the house.

I had just turned four and a half when we moved to this new place, and mom was already pregnant with my sister, Emily. Mike was seven, and soon after we moved into this rental house, my sister was born. Emily was born early in the morning one October day. On that morning, my dad came into our room and woke up my brother and me and told us mom just had a baby. I sat next to my mom and met my sister for the very first time. I was fascinated by her tiny little face; eyes closed with tongue sticking out tasting the world. She was the tiniest little thing I had ever seen in my life—very red with soft skin.

She smelled warm and sweet, like caramel and slept peacefully next to my mom, wrapped in a blanket.

Growing up, we always had a rescued dog in the family. We had a white dog named Lani once who was a mixture of Husky and Terrier. He was beautiful, strong, and loyal. My dad found him one day in a school where he used to work and brought him home. Lani played with me all the time, and wherever I went, he would follow. In the afternoons, Mom liked to sit outside the house and chat with her friends in the neighborhood while Lani and I would play on the street in front of our house.

There are certain characteristics animals possess that resemble that of human beings. They can be loyal, compassionate, authentic, generous, kind, and strong. Lani possessed all those traits—characteristics that reflected the kind of person I would want to be. Beautiful and soulful.

Lani stayed with the family for a very long time until one day mom found out she was pregnant with Emily. Dad said we couldn't have him anymore and needed to get rid of him.

"Get rid of him!?" I cried. "What do you mean, we have to get rid of him?"

"Well, he just can't stay with the family anymore," Dad said.

"Why not?" I asked.

"Because you are going to have a little sister and Lani has fleas," Dad said."He's dirty and it's not good for the baby."

"But why? I'm dirty too. We can wash him."

I never quite figured out why my parents had to let Lani go. I didn't understand the concept of letting go of something because you no longer see its value. I would like to think my parents had a good reason to let go of Lani, even if I couldn't see it.

"He's family, Daddy."

I pleaded with my dad and hoped he would change his mind and let Lani stay with us. I cried myself to sleep that night and surprisingly, it was as if Lani knew what was going to happen. He was awfully quiet that night and didn't come to say goodnight to me as he usually did.

The following night, Dad took Mike and me and Lani out for a ride on the motorbike.

It was a chilly night and my brother hadn't changed out of his khaki uniform from school. He was wearing an orange baseball cap with the school's logo in the middle of the hat. I was in my yellow polka-dot dress and Lani sat in his usual spot, right in the front of the motorbike at the foot rest space. It was dark when we got to the beach, but as we got closer to the water, I could make out the waves pushing up against the shore. The beach was surrounded by thick vegetation, with a few residential houses nearby.

"Lani, stay," Dad told him.

And then, just like that, Dad told us to get back on to the motorbike. My brother didn't say anything at all, but I was four years old at the time and I didn't understand why Dad would tell Lani to stay there.

Dad started his motorbike and I sat in the back, sandwiched between my Dad and my brother. I turned and watched Lani chasing after us. He wanted to come home; he kept chasing our motorbike, running and running and running until finally, he couldn't keep up with us anymore. I returned home crying, wanting Lani back, not understanding why my mom and dad would abandon Lani like that and why we couldn't have Lani around in the house. I'd never known what it was like to be abandoned by my own family or the feeling of being alone, but I remember seeing Lani chasing after the motorbike and the desperation in his eyes. I would never forget that look of abandonment. It would haunt me forever.

A few years later, Dad came home with another white dog that looked like Lani. Dad said it was Lani coming home to us. The dog had white fur just like Lani, and bluish eyes just like Lani, but I knew it wasn't him at all. This dog may have looked like Lani, but I knew deep down inside that it wasn't him. We left Lani by the beach, which we should have never done; we should have never abandoned him in the first place. Years later, even today, whenever I think about abandonment, Lani's eyes always come into my mind. The image of him chasing after us that night when we left him on the beach, the memory of how he used to play with us, watching over us and keeping us safe, the memory of having something and losing it gave me a taste of what it feels like to lose something close and precious.

We lived in this rental place for eight months before we bought a home of our very own. Our new three-story house was still being built back then when my dad first took my brother and me to see it. Then, it was just an empty building with drywall with nothing inside, no windows, no door, just the structure of a community home; our house was the fifth house in that row of buildings. It looked dull and boring, but Mike and I were still excited about moving into our new house because Dad said we would each get our own room.

"Can I decorate my room, Daddy?" I asked.

"Sure! anything you want," he said.

"Where is Emily going to sleep? Do I have to share my room with Emma?"

"She's still too small to have a room. You can have it all to yourself," Dad replied.

I imagined what my new room was going to look like. I had seen pink sheets and pillows at the department store before, and like the pink ones with flowers printed on them. I would love to have a teddy bear, too, or some kind of stuffed animal to hold on to at night when I went to sleep.

This new house we bought was surrounded by farmland, and I used to run with my brother and sister onto the rice fields after harvest. We dug holes in the ground and gathered dry weeds that we'd stuff into the holes, then light them with a match to start a small, contained fire. When the fire burned hot, we'd toss in some sweet potatoes, letting them bake inside the raw clay oven we'd just made in the ground. We ran with our neighbor kids till sunset, and we would each walk home with a freshly baked sweet potato.

Farmers didn't like us digging holes in the ground

and running around in their fields. Whenever they saw us on their property, they'd pick up their tools and chase us out. It was fun, exciting, and scary all at the same time. What if they caught us? What if we didn't get to dig out the sweet potatoes from the ground before the farmers brought us to our parents?

My parents fought about money from time to time throughout my childhood. When I was in the third grade—a time when the lottery first became big in Taiwan and Dad was intent on finding the right numbers like a mathematician every month—he spent a portion of his salary buying lottery tickets with his friends with the numbers he had figured out as a sure wins. He got lucky the first couple of times and won some money, but one day, Mom and Dad had a big fight. They were yelling and screaming at each other right in the middle of the living room.

"That was a month's salary!" Mom yelled across the living room while Dad was in the kitchen. "What do you expect us to do now?"

"I'm sorry," Dad said. "It won't happen again."

Dad started to walk toward the living room as he answered Mom in a soft voice. This, of course, did not settle Mom's boiling emotions, and she carried on questioning Dad's intentions and the logic behind them. At one point, she looked directly into my eyes and slowly walked to the kitchen to get things out of the refrigerator to cook.

"Jack told me this was going to be a big pot of money and I thought…." Dad went on explaining. But Mom was furious by now, having listened to enough of Dad's rationalizations. She was so angry that she grabbed a plate in front of her and smashed it to the floor, breaking it into pieces.

"You thought!? Well, guess what? You thought wrong! Now what? Do you expect me to take the kids and we all die together? Is that what you thought of?"

Dad didn't say much, and went to get a broom and dustpan, telling us not to put our bare feet on the floor until he cleaned up the mess. Later on, I heard my mom say that Dad had used the entire month's budget to buy those lottery ticket and that she would never forgive him for using family money to gamble.

I was scared when Mom got this angry. She'd always been strong, but in a very loving way. I remember seeing her losing herself one time. I must have been five or six years old. Dad came into the bedroom and found mom passed out after drinking a whole bottle of whisky.

Dad didn't make much money; he taught at a private high school, but unlike other teachers at his school who sometimes accepted bribes from parents, Dad worked hard for every penny he earned. He never brought home any "gifts" or bribes from parents of students wanting advance placements. Dad had what people would call "integrity," but Mom called it "stupidity."

"Look how far you have gotten us," Mom said.

Every time my parents fought, it usually had something to do with money. Sometimes my dad would come home very drunk from his social gatherings. Because our financial situation was not an easy one, Mom ended up opening a beauty parlor in our home, in an enclosed patio overlooking the front yard. Many families, as ours did, in Taiwan remodel their home by removing the old cracked mud plaster, replastering the walls on the inside and out, then whitewashing or painting them. That's what we did. Mom and dad also extended our house by fencing off a couple of extra square feet in front of our house with bricks and concrete to create a private area that was separate from our family's communal space. Mirrors were then mounted onto the wall, a red armchair installed for customers to sit on, a sink to wash and rinse their hair, and finally, some basic hairstyling supplies completed the salon.

When Dad came home really drunk, Mom would leave him out in the front-yard patio/salon, lock the doors, and tell everyone to go to bed. Dad would often end up passed out on the red armchair. When he was drunk, he talked a lot. I would watch him from a window inside the house and could smell him every time he turned or mumbled something, a combination of alcohol and vomit.

"I....I ammmm OK; I ammmm not druuuunk," Dad slurred loudly.

"Of course, you are not! Even though you could barely walk when you came in through the door," Mom replied while hastening to close the door.

"You stay out there! You can vomit all you want! I am not cleaning you up," she insisted. "Next time, don't bother coming home!"

The next morning when Dad woke up, he

generally did not remember anything that had transpired the night before. Mom wouldn't speak to him for a few days and sometimes I imagined that one day I might wake up and neither of my parents would be around anymore. They might have gotten a divorce and left me.

My mom described me as a very quiet baby. The day that I was born, I laid in the crib, tiny hands and feet, eyes roaming around the ceiling, observing the world as it was. She said I turned out to be a happy baby, easy to care for, and didn't require much in the way of attention. From time to time, she would reminisce about the day I was born, when she delivered me at the home of a midwife. Next to her was another woman giving birth to a baby boy. "He was loud!" she said, scrunching her eyebrows. "He wouldn't stop crying the whole time."

There's something unique about what the eyes don't see. On the surface, I looked just like every other baby in the world, but underneath that was something special. Have you ever walked into a garden full of roses, and picked just *one* out of all the possible flowers? What makes that rose so special? Because you know that no matter how similar appearances look, there are characteristics that make everything and everyone unique. Sure, I may look like every other baby in this world on the outside, but inside, there was something special about me.

My mom was a stay-at-home parent and I used to follow her around the house watching her do household chores. In the morning, she would go to the street market and get fresh vegetables and other groceries to prepare our meals for the day. I would ride with her on the motorbike and sometimes she would take me to watch a movie at the cinema. She liked scary movies, and I would sit beside her in the darkened theater, frightened and eyes closed, as the scary scenes lit up the big screen.

Almost in direct contrast to her love of horror films, Mom was also a skilled knitter. She once knitted me a skirt of red yarn. I loved that skirt and wore it every week for a very long time. One day I noticed my skirt was too short, barely covering my underpants, and there was a small hole on the lower right side, just big enough to fit my pinkie through it. But I loved that skirt so much that I couldn't just throw it away. Instead, I left it in my dresser.

My parents are big believers in education. My mom, who was the eldest of four siblings, quit school at age 16. In Taiwanese culture, it's not uncommon for families to divert all financial resources to the kids who show the most intellectual promise, while encouraging less academically inclined offspring to start working to provide for themselves. My mom did not quite fit in the category of being the smartest kid in her family, so, at the age of 16, she left home and went to Taipei, the capital of Taiwan, and found a job at a textile mill.

Even though my mom only finished seventh grade, she is a woman with a lot of wisdom. She likes to read novels, listen to radio talk shows, and she always has a curiosity about new things. There's a quote that goes, "The best teacher in life is your own experience." My mom embodied this philosophy fully in her life. She learned through her life experiences.

I hardly ever see my mom cry, although she does get very emotional when she watches television dramas. There were times I caught her watching some television drama, and she would cry over the weirdest things. One day she was watching a talk show on the topic of politics, and a guest on the show was describing a story about leaving her marriage because she didn't receive the support she needed from her husband when she fought with her mother-in-law, and how she went on to become a political influencer. As the woman described the day she left her marriage, Mom started to cry. It was as if she was that woman on the show describing her own circumstances.

There were qualities in my mom that I saw, even at a very young age, that made me want to be like her when I grew up, especially her inner strength. My grandparents always favored my aunt Shelly. Aunt Shelly is the second child in their family, and always liked school and did well academically. And because Aunt Shelly needed to study for school, my grandparents would assign all the household chores to my mom. What I noticed about my mom was her ability to cope in any type of situation. She never complained, never said "No" to my grandparents, and she never disobeyed them in any way.

A few years ago, when Grandpa passed away, Mom finally said it out loud. "I knew I was not as smart as Aunt Shelly. This is why I had to do all those things for your grandpa and grandma—because Aunt Shelly needed to study, and Grandpa favored her over me. I never got the love from him I needed, and I know your Grandpa knew that as well. Last night when he passed, he told me he was sorry."

The strength of a woman is not measured by the impact of her hardships in life, but through finding her voice and the strength to her refuse to allow those hardships to dictate who she becomes. That's my mom. She is full of strength and determination. Growing up, I was always more intimidated by my mom than by my dad. My dad was much more lenient with us, and we could get away with things more easily with him than with Mom.

There is an old Chinese palm-reading myth that says if the lifeline within a woman's palm is positioned in such a way that it splits her palm in half, she is going to live a hard life and that those around her will also face hardships. It wasn't until my teenage years that I discovered the lines on both of my mom's palms are configured that way. Sometimes I wonder whether this is just an old wives' tale or whether there's some truth to it. I always knew my mom was the tough one in the house.

When Mom gets angry, we take it very, very seriously. When she's mad, you don't dare say a word, because she will smack the shit out of you.

When I was in the second grade, I was supposed to learn how to count money. Mom sat me down that summer before school started, took money out of her purse, and laid it out in front of me.

"How much is this?" she asked, taking out a $20 bill, three quarters, and a nickel.

"….Twenty-five?" I suggested.

Bam! She hit me with the back of her hair brush.

"Count it again!" she told me.

"…Twenty…"

She hit me again.

I was crying, wiping my nose. I really tried hard to add the numbers up. But for some reason I could never get them to add up to $20.80. By the end of that summer, I still didn't know how to count money. Heck! Even to this day, I have trouble counting money. But when I think about this a little more, that's probably why they invented the calculator.

Finally, Mom gave up on me, having concluded that math and I were just not a good match together. I never liked math— a subject I just scraped by in at school. One day when I was in the fourth grade, I came home with a score of 38 on my math test. It was so horrible that I folded that test paper into my school bag, only holding my high-scoring test papers from other classes in my hand.

"Mom, look! I got a 98 on my language test!"

"Where are the rest of your test papers?"

Of course, she had to ask, right?

"Well, yeah. I got 38 on math."

At some point, my mom got tired of hitting us. Every time we behaved badly, she would send us to the corner of the living room and tell us to kneel for hours.

Both of my parents were strict, but I never considered those moments abusive. I saw them as a form of discipline. Through my dad's experiences in the military, I learned to keep my bedroom clean, my sheets folded, my clothes ironed, and all my homework and school books neatly prepared in my bookbag for the next day. And my mom didn't hit us just for the sake of it; she hit us because this is what Chinese culture is like; our culture was built on rules and authority. And in many ways, it worked. I grew up having a good amount of self-control in all areas of my life and it served me really well.

Despite my dad's decision to abandon our dog at the beach, gambling with the family budget, and being drunk after social events, he is actually quite family-oriented. Every night he preferred to have dinner with everyone sitting together at the table. He liked doing things as a family, traveling together, and eating together.

Every weekend he would drive us back to my grandparents' house to visit his side of the family. My grandfather migrated to Taiwan during the resettlement of Kuomintang after Chinese Civil War in the 1940s. My paternal grandfather served in the military for Kuomintang as a sergeant. In the earlier days, everyone lived together in a veteran community. My dad came from a family of four and, like me, is the second child in his family.

Going to the grandparents' house meant a number

of things, including getting to see all of my cousins. Often, my older cousins would look after us when we went to a nearby store to buy snacks and candy. We also had a few hang-outs around the neighborhood—old abandoned dugouts that were used during the anti-Japanese War of Resistance and World War II. These were air-raid shelters left over from the early 1930s, and some of the veteran villages kept them in case of another war. Occasionally, when we'd hear the siren ringing through the speakers at the local community office, we got to practice using them. My cousins and I would spend time at these dugouts and also exploring the village.

Before my paternal grandfather joined the Army, his family owned land for farming. But my grandfather was not much of a farmer; he was more of a military type of person who did everything by the book; very disciplined and sturdy. I hardly had any interaction with him when I was growing up, since he was not the type of person to mingle with children. Now that I think of it, my dad resembles him a lot. He'd been a smoker his entire life, and every memory I have of him is of him sitting with friends and family playing Mahjong with one hand, and flicking a cigarette into the ashtray beside him with the other. My grandfather had a shed in the back of the house where he kept all his tools, and next to the shed was this big, old guava tree. Every time we'd visit the grandparents' house, my cousin, my brother, and I would climb up into the tree and pick perfectly ripe guava straight from the tree. Sometimes my brother would climb to the roof of the shed with one of my cousins and lay there napping in the afternoons.

There were routines that I watched my dad perform that I believed were really good habits. For example, every night before he'd go to sleep, he'd take out his Army uniform and make sure it was clean and ironed. He polished his shoes every now and then and, while he ate, always brought his bowl to his mouth rather than mouth to the bowl. He'd sit straight, walk tall, and had beautiful handwriting that I admired when I was little. I also learned a few things from him about saving money. I used to keep all the empty cookie boxes and would cut out a little slot to deposit coins, transforming them into a piggy banks for myself. Every day, my mom would give me snack money and I would save this money in the cookie-box bank I made for myself.

In second grade, I started to participate in speech contests at school. My dad was a good writer and would sometimes spend nights writing speeches for me. My job was easy; I just had to memorize my speech, go up to the stage, and deliver that speech as if I was the one who wrote it. Stagefright was not something I would experience. In fact, I really enjoyed being a performer. I volunteered myself every chance I got to be on stage singing and dancing, and I liked people telling me how good I was at each. It made me really proud.

My dad was very crafty, and he also liked the fact that there was a little performer in the house. Among my siblings and I, I had always been the one with more artistic skills. I remember one day Dad made me a little drum out of a tin can, and he made a cross-body strap to go with it. I wore it in the house, and danced while drumming it. Every once in a while, I would sing for the family. When home karaoke machines first became available where we lived, my dad knew he needed to get one for me. I'd picked up a lot of oldies from hearing my mom sing; singing came naturally for me, and my sister and I used to do a lot of pretend-performing. We would wear old sheets, which I'd transform into long "hair" and pretend I was a superstar. On those rainy days when we weren't in school, I'd stand on our couch performing before my sister and an imaginary crowd.

It wasn't until years later that I started to realize that my childhood memories were somewhat vague and fragmented. While many people can recall memories from the age of five or six years old, often I can recall only pieces of them. They are like fragments of scenes cobbled together; sometimes they make sense, and sometimes they are just hazy.

Growing up, Emily and I were always closer than we were to our brother Mike. Still, Mom said that I almost killed Emily one time when I was four years old. It was an average day for me at age four; Mom stepped out to run errands and left Emily and me in the room during our nap. When I awoke, my sister was crying. She cried and cried and cried, and I must have gotten annoyed by her nagging cry, so I picked up a pile of clothing from the side of our bed and I placed it right on top of her face in an attempt to quiet her. Luckily, Mom came in just in time and quickly removed the clothes and picked Emily up. But this story still gets around in my house every now and then, including the Mom brought it up when my sister brought her would-be husband over for the first time.

There's something about memories that, no matter how sweet or painful they are, play an important part within our lives. It's almost like having an invisible box we carry with us everywhere as we navigate the river of life. In this box, we keep all of our secrets, stories, shadows, and light; it is also the box that keeps our hearts brave and our minds strong. It is where we keep ourselves warm inside, and it beats like a second heart. There were a lot of memories I kept inside my box; all my joys and sorrows, all my light and shadows, and all my good days and bad days.

Every morning my brother Mike would dress for school in his khaki uniform, orange cap, and blue shorts. I always wanted to do the same—to be able to go to school wearing uniform and have homework to do after school. I thought it was really cool to watch him coming home with books and notes to read.

When I started first grade three years later, I finally got my chance to enjoy that tedious process of preparing oneself toward a bigger goal. I can still see myself sitting in front of my desk, opening my textbook, and reviewing what I learned in school that day. I'd read each text line by line and practice writing words in my workbook; turning them into sentences and making sure to include every punctuation mark. At bedtime, I put away my textbooks and workbook along with the small dictionary I carried in my bookbag, arranging them so they were perfectly aligned and organized.

Beside enjoying academic work, I was also very outgoing and active in school. I've always known I had that ability to lead others, and at school, kids would follow me around during recess and listen to me as though I was someone important. Classmates would gather around my desk waiting to speak to me, and we would talk about our adventures in the schoolyard, what we learned that day, and, sometimes, they would invite me to join them on the swings, where I would assign them specific roles.

"You, run to the swings and take two swings before anyone else gets to them," I told my classmate Jenny.

"Okay! I will save one for you," Jenny replied.

Jenny usually sat in the back of the classroom because she was really tall compared to the other third grade students. I used her geographic advantage—the fact she sat closest to the door—which meant she could run out of the classroom to the playground the fastest. And then there was Robert, who was chubby with really curly short hair, a native Taiwanesse with indigenous looks. Robert always seemed to be happy. Nothing really bothered him, and he'd always follow me around like a lost puppy. I didn't mind Robert, though, because he often made me laugh.

I liked that feeling of being important and

being seen. There was a part of me that enjoyed the attention from my classmates. Every recess I'd gather kids from my class by a big giant oak tree in the school yard where I would give commands for them to follow. Each person would take turns on the swing and we would then rotate to play hopscotch. During lunch breaks we would walk together to a nearby shop outside of school and watch television together until the school bell rang again.

One day we were all gathering around the tree during recess. It rained heavily the day before and there were puddles everywhere. I am not sure what got into me but we were so involved in playing together that I obviously felt I did not need to go use the restroom when I really needed to. I kept holding it and holding it, and finally by the time I made it to the bathroom, it was too late. My pants didn't come off fast enough and there I was, wet in my pants.

"What do I do?" I thought to myself. I walked over to a sink, turned on the faucet, and let the water run down my pants. I was hoping to wash away the smell. At that moment, a feeling of shame overwhelmed me, so I came up with what I thought was the best solution to the problem: I lied.

The recess bell had rung and students were heading back to their classrooms, so I went back into my classroom and told the teacher I slipped, and that I needed to call my mom so she could bring a change of clothes for me. My mom came to school with some dry clothes and asked me what happened. I was ashamed, so I lied again.

"We were playing, and I slipped."

She didn't ask any more questions after I changed, but that moment stayed with me, just her and me in a small boiler room in school. She took my wet pants home and I went back to the classroom pretending that was exactly what happened, but I could still smell the urine that ran down my pants as I stood there in the bathroom thinking, "what should I do?" I'll never forget that smell.

My elementary school was established in 1980, a year before I enrolled in first grade in '81. It sat in the middle of a large rice farm surrounded by vast empty space. The front gate led to a main road which then merged onto a busy main street at a crossroads. On one side of the street were shops, restaurants, and residential houses. On the other side of the street, smaller roads branched off, leading to another residential area.

I met my best friend, Hui, in the third grade. We were both very petite, and on the first day of school, we were all gathered outside the classroom and lined up into five rows. This was the way we were assigned seats in the classroom, with the shorter students lined up at the front and the taller students in the back. Hui and I ended up in the front every year. She always sat in the seat next to mine, and we shared the same desk.

She's the oldest one in her family and she had an accident when she was little that caused nerve damage in her face, making her eyebrows and face twitch when she spoke. I didn't mind that at all, but sometimes boys in our class would make fun of her and imitate her facial spasms. She was very smart, and we were ranked after each exam throughout the year and she would always rank at number one.

One year, there was another boy in our class, Jimmy, who was also really smart. The two of them always ranked at the top of our class academically, and it felt almost as if there was a competition between the two of them. I felt special having Hui as my best friend because other classmates assumed that since Hui was really smart, I must be, too. But I knew it wasn't true. I knew I would never be number one in my class like Jimmy and Hui, but I still had that feeling of "I'm walking around with the smartest person in the class" and therefore, people saw me differently.

This is a very common interpretation people carry with them, thinking that if you hang out with smart people, you probably excel, too. To some degree, this is true, and there's a lot of evidence to support the idea that "like attracts like." Psychologists even encourage people to find their own tribe, knowing we thrive when we're with like-minded people. I felt that in the third grade—like I was being treated differently, in a good way, because of Hui.

I learned a few things from her during those years. The first thing I noticed that was special about her was her beautiful Chinese calligraphy handwriting. It was almost the same caliber you would see in framed prints. She sat next to me in class and it was hard not to notice her handwriting. I watched her lay each word down in her workbook, filling out the boxes with perfect Chinese characters. I was fascinated and wanted to be like her. Coming home from school that day, I sat at my desk, picked up my pen, and—one stroke at a time—I, too, learned to write gracefully in my workbook.

You know how sometimes we see great qualities in someone else and want to emulate those qualities in ourselves? That was me watching my best friend writing those characters in her workbook; I wanted to be just like her. This admiration was so strong that at one point, I even started to imitate her twitchy facial expressions. Hui was also good at writing. In writing class, she would always come up with articles that were beautifully constructed and use vocabulary that I had never even heard before. Things just seemed so easy for her. In a way, I felt a bit jealous of her talents.

One day I asked her how she learned to write so well, and she pulled out a book and showed it to me. She told me that she read a lot, besides studying our textbook when she goes home, and that she reads books to learn words and phrases that she could use in her writing. After school that day, I asked my mom to take me to a book shop, where I got a book similar to the one Hui had showed me, and I went home and began reading it.

Hui's house was just a few hundred feet from the school. Her dad was a rice farmer and they lived in a very traditional house. She would run home sometimes during our lunch break to eat at home rather than at school. On hot summer days, Hui and I would run across the rice field and cut across everyone else chasing each other to the main street. I liked the smell of the grass, and the trees dancing as the wind howled, watching the breeze blow through, sparking joy and hope in me. There was the shop on the corner of the street where we would watch TV for an hour during our lunch break. This was also where I'd wait for my mom to pick me up from school. Usually, Mom would drive her motorbike and wait for us at the school gate, but if she was running late, Hui and I would take a short walk and meet my mom by this corner shop. We didn't know then what was to come, and I had no idea how much I would miss those days.

Chapter

Two

"It's really a wonder that I haven't dropped all my ideals, because they seem so absurd and impossible to carry out. Yet I keep them, because in spite of everything, I still believe that people are really good at heart."

— Anne Frank, *The Diary of a Young Girl*

I t began as an ordinary summer day. I was 11 by now, and had just started fifth grade. Mom was running late, and wasn't there waiting at the gate for me after school. Hui and I started toward the corner shop. We took a shortcut across the farmland to the main street like we often did, then waited on the same side of the street, in front of the shop. Hui and I sat there on the patio for a while, watching the traffic ebb and flow. Student volunteers from the senior classes were directing traffic, with a teacher standing on the side of the street, supervising.

This intersection could be very busy at times, and during school hours, four senior class members would bring their equipment out and stand two on each side holding a long bamboo stick with warning signs to stop traffic to allow students to cross the street safely.

"That looks really fun," I thought. "When I get to the senior class, that's what I will ask to do. I want to be directing traffic like that."

I turned to Hui sitting next to me as I was observing this and told her that she could be my counterpart. She liked the idea and we both came up with some brilliant idea of changing the warning sign to make it bigger and brighter. We looked into each other's eyes and both started to laugh.

In the distance, I saw my mom riding her motorbike in our direction. I told Hui I was going to wait for my mom across the street. The seniors helping direct traffic just finished their work, and had gathered on one corner of the crossing, ready to head back to the school with their supervising teacher. There were still children walking leisurely out of school and chatting to each other, laughing, playing; a typical after-school scene.

The main street is not an extremely busy street, but traffic could be heavy at times, especially back in the old days, when there wasn't a traffic lights installed at this intersection. Our teacher, Jasmine, told us that, the week before, a student was hurt crossing the street.

"Luckily, he was OK. there were just some minor scratches on him," she said.

After that accident, our principal, Mr. Kwan, made an announcement during our morning ceremony. Mr. Kwan asked the students from the senior class to make sure not to leave early when they were assigned to direct traffic. "This will help the school ensure all students are safe," he said. Everyone applauded.

As I ran across the intersection, I turned and waved goodbye to Hui. Out of the corner of my eye, I thought I saw something coming towards me. I saw Hui stand up from her bench and I heard some students who were still on the other side yelling, "STOP! STOP!" I found myself standing in the middle of the street, turning to get a sense of what was going on. Suddenly, I heard the deafening sound of screeching tires. I could smell burning rubber, and there was smoke emanating from somewhere, but I couldn't tell which direction it was coming from. I panicked, not knowing which way to turn. Then there was a loud thud followed by complete darkness.

I woke up in a hospital with no memory of how I got there. The only things that were clear were the agony of my mother's cry, my father's look of desperation, and the doctor wearing his white coat standing next to us. I felt a lot of discomfort in my lower extremities and, asked where my brother was.

"He's coming; he'll be here in a minute," Dad replied.

I wasn't really sure why I had asked for my brother except that I just wanted to see some familiar faces. There was a tremendous amount of fear rising within me waking up in a hospital like this—so completely foreign. It was at that moment I realized that my life was about to change, whether I was ready or not.

At the hospital, I was wrapped with plaster from the waist down. I couldn't move because it had stabilized my hip area, making me look like I was wearing cement pants. The doctor in charge told me that I was fortunate, and it was "just a few broken bones." But little did we know at the time that it wasn't "just a few broken bones." It was the day that completely changed the way I live, as well as all of those around me. It was the day I lost my chance to live a normal life, and it was a day I wished I could go back and change every single moment of.

You know how life sometimes puts us in a spot in which we don't have much of a choice? We were born with certain features and characteristics; we didn't ask for these but somehow, they were just given to us. The way we look, the shape of our noses, the size of our eyes, how tall we're going to be. We blame it on life for throwing those lemons at us when we did not ask for them. Well, I blamed the intersection for not having traffic lights installed. I blamed Mom for running late that day and instead of picking me up at the front door, making me cross the street to meet her.

Oftentimes, we blame everyone else but ourselves for the things that don't go very well in our lives.

Instead of taking responsibility for our choices and coming up with solutions, what do we do? In most cases, we sit and dwell on how unfortunate we are for having to experience life's agonies, but in fact, it is we, ourselves, who are 100 percent responsible for our own destinies.

The fact is that I made a choice that day to run across the street while I was distracted. The taxi driver made a choice by speeding and driving recklessly. Mom made a choice by arriving late to pick me up. And I made a choice about what my life was going to look like from that day forward. We are constantly making choices in our everyday lives and, depending on how you perceive the outcomes, you may be a victim of your own thoughts rather than a victim of circumstances. Which is worse? I don't know.

In that 11-year-old body of mine, I was trapped in my own tragedy. The tragedy of how I perceived this accident and what I had lost. I was trapped in my own drama.

After being discharged from the ER, my parents brought me home. They set up a bed in the living room since I wasn't able to go upstairs to my bedroom. I needed to be carried everywhere I went. My parents brought their mattresses downstairs and we all slept in the living room at night during my initial recovery. It was kind of fun; how often do parents allow their children to make a mess in their living room? How often do you get to sleep together with your parents at night? And how often do you camp right in your own living room? There was part of me that was feeling glad that this happened because it meant I didn't have to go to school for a while and I could stay home watching TV all the time.

Imagine being 11 years old, bedridden, with a plaster cast on a hot summer day. There was nothing to do. I could only move six inches to the side of the bed rail. The only fun activity was watching TV, reading books, and drawing. The first few weeks were tolerable, but I had to do this for the next three months, until my bones healed and grew again. I was anxious, angry, and bitter. I commanded my seven-year-old sister to get my water, pick up my bedpan, and bring me the TV remote control, and much more. I was a very bossy big sister.

Mom tried to accommodate my emotions and boredom as much as she could. She tried hard to keep me entertained so I wouldn't have to think about how uncomfortable it was to exist in this plaster cast. She bought me a diary. It was small, about three inches by four inches in size, pink with floral detail and a little lock on the outside and a key to open it up.

She found it when she was out grocery shopping one day. Before my accident, she would take me with her to the street market near our house where we would buy fresh meat and vegetables. Once in a while, I'd get to buy something small from one of the market vendors, but ever since the accident, I couldn't go to the market with her anymore. Every morning, she would leave me home alone for a few hours while she went to the market to get groceries. She made sure I had plenty of things to do before she left. On the day she came home with the diary, and I opened it up and the smell of perfume wafted out. As I turned each page, the fragrance floated up to my nose. It was the first time that I started keeping a journal. I kept many of my thoughts in those pages, and kept writing in that journal until my first year of high school when all the pages started to fall apart.

Besides the diary, my parents bought other stuff for me during those three long, difficult months. One day, Mom came home with two mini rabbits from the street market. She was really excited to show me; she opened the box and I saw two tiny white faces staring out from the cardboard box. I was really excited to feed them cabbage, watch them eat, and even poop in their box. The guy who sold the "mini rabbits" to my mom had, however, lied to her. They weren't mini rabbits at all; they grew up to be gigantic, regular size rabbits. As they grew and grew, I could no longer keep them in the living room or in their box. We ended up setting up a corner on the roof to house these now-enormous rabbits.

Everyone knows rabbits like to jump, and our rabbits were no exception. One day, one of them jumped onto the fence surrounding the roof and almost fell off. And there were so many rabbit droppings that my parents became tired of cleaning and feeding them. Mom and Dad came up with a permanent solution to this problem: let's just eat the rabbits. And so we did.

While I was bed-bound, I watched a lot of TV; from cartoons to television drama series and movies.

One of the most memorable movies my mom made me watch was a story about a man who was born a cripple, yet who worked his way up through education and hard work. Though disadvantaged and discriminated against out in the world, he also had support from loved ones in his endeavors. This is how it's supposed to be right? I watch someone else's story and am supposed to believe that my situation isn't so bad, or that I am not as unfortunate as someone else, and that I should be grateful that I am still alive and be thankful for it. I did not see it that way. Instead of focusing on things that I still had, I focused on all the things I had lost.

In those moments, I imagined how it would be if none of life's tragedies had happened. I would have been just like everyone else, living a normal life, going to school, playing with my friends, running and jumping and enjoying life. The movie wasn't bad; I could see how being born with a handicap could be hard, but it didn't relate to how I was feeling inside. Oftentimes we look at other people's misfortunes and think to ourselves, "I should be grateful for what I have." But how can anyone else's tragedy negate our own? It can't.

One day, my fifth-grade teacher, Mr. Hou, came to visit me at home. He was an amazing human being, extremely talented and wise, and in his early forties. He played sports and coached our soccer team, and he also taught physical education at our school. I was also enrolled in his Chinese calligraphy class. Mr. Hou came over and sat beside my bed along with my mom and asked, "What do you want to be in 10 years?"

He looked into my eyes and waited for me to give him an answer. I didn't know how to respond. I was so rooted in my personal sorrow that I didn't think I had the answer to that question. I was caught up with what had happened and the fact that I was here, bedridden, unable to move, to go to school, or to play with friends outside. I was focused on the little drama that I created in my world. I stared back into his eyes feeling frazzled. I didn't know what to say, or rather, I could not comprehend what he meant.

"What happened to you was an accident. No one wanted it to happen, but it did," he said. "Think about yourself 10 years from today. What do you want to do and where do you want to be?"

Mr. Hou was not the only teacher in my life to inspire me to broaden my outlook to recognize and connect with something larger than myself.

My teacher Jasmine, whom I'd had since second grade, was very gentle and graceful, always wore a blouse with a skirt that fell below her knee. She was tall and had long hair, and when she walked, her hair would sweep from side to side. Usually, though, she wore it in a bun, twisting her hair together and holding it up with a clip. Her teaching style was very soft and kind. Whenever I think of the quintessential teacher, the image of her always came up in my memory. I always wanted to be a teacher, to be someone like her. I remember I used to roleplay with kids from my neighborhood; we had this little blackboard at home, and I would have all the kids around the neighborhood sit down in front of me and have them write down words, tell them to repeat after me, and act as if I was a real teacher.

There was always a part of me inside that wanted to be seen and be heard. I wanted to be somebody, and I wanted to be someone who lead and taught others.

Being home and bedridden at age 11 was not a pleasant experience. I kept wondering what friends were doing in school; what are they learning today? What homework did they have? Who is becoming whose friend, and who is missing me while I'm gone? Do they talk about me and remember me at all?

My mom asked my teacher to send me books and supplies so I could work at home. I was able to read from the textbook but no one came to offer me home-schooling. Having those textbooks at home was the closest thing I could get to being in a classroom. Sometimes I imagined myself waking up in the morning with things just the way they used to be before the accident, but instead, I spent that summer in bed, trapped.

When the weather turned hot, I'd feel itchy and sweaty. It was not comfortable being immobilized in plaster from the waist down. When my calf would get itchy, I was unable to scratch it and it was almost unbearable. Eventually, I became very creative when it came to scratching those itches. My mom got me some knitting rods and I'd extend them between my body and the plaster cast to get to the itch. The worst experience in life is having an itch that you can't get to. It drove me nuts!

On rainy days, I would lie in bed and spend hours listening to the rain pouring down on the roof panels. Other days, I'd listen to the cicadas sing. They'd come out in droves during the summer. We didn't have an air conditioner at the time—those were still expensive to buy—so Mom would turn on the fan in the living room and put a bamboo sheet beneath me to help cool me off. When it was quiet enough, all I could hear were the cicadas' loud chorus. Of course, I didn't know at the time that this could be a form of meditation, whereby you tune in to ambient sounds, focusing on nothing else. I found tranquility and joy in those moments. I also read a lot during those long, sweaty summer days. My mom borrowed a lot of books for me to distract me and keep me entertained. That summer I must have read the entire series of Arsene Lupin crime-solving mystery books.

After the plaster cast was removed at the end of that summer, I was pretty sure all my friends from school would have forgotten who I was. No one had ever bothered to call me, write to me, or come by to visit. And everyone at school was getting ready to move up to sixth grade, and sooner or later, they would be graduating. As for me, I was sent to physical rehabilitation center in Taipei by my parents for further recovery. It was run by the wife of Generalissimo and President Chiang Kai-Shek, Madame Chiang Kai-shek, the first lady of the Republic of China. The rehabilitation center housed children from the age of five until the adolescent years. It consisted of a surgery center, physical therapy center, and on-site school for kindergarteners, and skills-training for young adolescents. Admission fees were waived for military families, and in my case, my dad made us eligible so I was able to receive care without added financial burden to my family.

The patients' rooms were divided into different sections, each with six beds for six patients. Three in each row and another three across the room. It was an open floor plan, and each of us could see everyone else, and everyone eventually ended up *knowing* everyone else, too. Family members were not allowed on-site and visitation was only given during the week of surgery or on weekends. The rehab center had two buildings, one old and the other newer. And anything new is always better, right? That rule applies here as well. Everyone wanted to be in the new building rather than the old one.

The first night my parents dropped me off at the rehabilitation center, I was wearing a yellow dress with green polka dots. I loved that dress very much. I was admitted and placed into the old building where most younger patients from ages six to 12 would live. There weren't too many patients within my unit. Each of us was assigned a small cabinet where we could leave our personal belongings, as well as a metal bed topped with a thin layer of foam mattress.

My first day there, my parents stayed as long as they could, until it was getting really late. Home was miles away from Taipei and it would take them a good hour and a half of driving to get there. When my parents left that day, for the first time in my life, I suddenly felt a sense of loneliness. I didn't know what to do. There was a sense of loss, disconnection, and abandonment within me, but I also knew they were doing what they believed was best. But still, I felt alone. Nurses were really nice and because it was my first time away from home with strangers, so they invited me to sit with them so I wouldn't feel as lonely. I sat across from the nurse's station and watched people going by and the nurses hard at work, but no one was really there *with* me.

I sat there for a while until finally it was time for me to shower and get ready for bed. I took out the little basket my parents had bought me along with my toothbrush and towel and proceeded to wash myself, brush my teeth, and change into the pajamas my mom bought me. It was a long-sleeve, purple cotton sleeping gown that hung to the floor, with a little light pink bow at the neck. I went to bed, but the detachment syndrome I experienced was so powerful that it kept me awake the whole night.

Lying in bed, I opened my eyes and noticed a window right above my bed. I could see the moon from that window, bright and so beautiful, beaming right onto my bed. All the other kids were sound asleep. I sat up and the room was so bright that I couldn't fall back to sleep because of homesickness. So, I sat there for a while and looked around me. There were some empty beds in my unit and things looked so unfamiliar that all of a sudden, I felt a sense of overwhelming sadness. I must have fallen asleep eventually, because I found myself waking up in the middle of this sensation, panicking. I felt devastated by the fact that I was alone.

"I want to go home," was my first thought. I wanted to be with my mom. That sense of missing home was so strong that I found myself pulling out my yellow polka-dot dress and changing out of my pajamas and into the dress as quietly as I could without waking my roommates. I packed my bag and I sat by the railing of the bed, sobbing, silently, knowing there was no one at that moment to come and save me.

My parents came the next day to check on me and to speak with the head doctor in charge of my care. They talked about the X-rays of my legs and how they weren't growing straight because of the ER doctor's negligence. They discussed what surgeries, from my hip to my shin, that they would need to perform in order to correct those. I thought it was just going to be a temporary recovery and that I would be able to go back to school soon to join the rest of my classmates for graduation. But things didn't go as I had imagined.

Living in a dormitory-style rehab center has its advantages and disadvantages. The disadvantages are that there isn't much privacy, and life can be boring sometimes without a living room to watch TV in and without places to go at night. The advantages are that you find a tribe of people coming together, you figure out how best to cohabitate. In our dorm, we understood each other. We could see and hear each other. I felt safe, and seeing other people who endured even more detrimental experiences than I had gave me a chance to see life differently. Finding my own tribe here was important; it was about connecting with people from familiar backgrounds who shared similar experiences and goals. Up until the age of 15, I lived on-site in this rehabilitation center in the Taiwanese capital.

One of the most popular events after dark in Taiwan is to hit one of the many night markets where you'll find lots of food vendors, clothing stalls, and sometimes exotic delicacies. Within walking distance of the rehabilitation center was a night market, and one of the most exciting adventures was going to the market as a group. My hospital roommates and I must have been quite a sight: a cluster of people in wheelchairs, rolling themselves down the street toward the night market, chatting, laughing, and socializing together. There was a bond that formed through our daily interactions. This is where we thrived, and where we allowed ourselves to become vulnerable and open our hearts to allow healing and recovery. This was a community.

Some of the stories I heard at the rehab center were happier than others; some demonstrated resilience, while others were more tragic. One of my roommates was this little girl, Yu. She was younger than me—I was 11 and going on 12 and she was just seven years old when we met. She looked especially small for her age: thin, skinny, a body of literal skin and bone. But what was different about her was her legs. Mom said she had some kind of tumor growing on her and that's why her legs looked big and floppy. Sometimes I caught myself staring at her and wondering what had happened to her. And I'd sometimes catch myself judging the way she looked. The size of the tumors on both of her legs were bigger than her two arms put together.

Yu was always quiet and didn't say much. I think she knew I was staring at her, so she glared back angrily. Her grandmother was always there to take care of her. Sometimes I'd think she was just a little spoiled brat, having seen her get very angry and abusive toward her grandmother. Yu would hit her grandmother when she did something that was not to her liking.

"I said, give me that paper!" Yu yelled.

"This one?" her grandmother replied.

"NO! that one over there." Yu pointed to the nightstand at the other side of the room while throwing the paper in her hand at grandmother's face.

I felt bad for her grandmother because she was older—probably in her seventies. Yu had a sister a few years younger than she was who looked just like her—tiny with short hair. Her sister, who was five at the time,and her mom came to visit her sometimes while her grandmother insisted on staying and sleeping overnight with her. For a while I was jealous of that because I wished my mom could stay and sleep over with me. "What makes her so special?" I thought.

We shared the same room, though she and her grandmother could be selfish when it came to sharing common spaces. Yu's grandmother could be very mean at times; there were incidents where other patients' families moved or touched the cooking pot she brought from home and she would yell at them. Needless to say, they didn't have a lot of friends.

I didn't understand what death meant at that time, but I knew it must be a painful thing. Everything about life and death I knew from watching television. I had never seen or heard of anyone dying before. I remember asking my mom once why Yu was so skinny and her legs were so big. Mom said it was because Yu's tumor was eating away all the nutrition from her. It reminded me of these sci-fi television shows where an alien or monster feeds on human flesh. I would sometimes watch Yu moving from her wheelchair onto her bed, swinging her legs like people swing their pillows. There were nights I watched her cry because of her pain, which I supposed was how you feel when the monster on your leg starts eating into your bones. I had also observed her grandmother crying through those painful times, seeing someone she loved moving toward death with each moment. I witnessed this and took it into my heart, telling myself, "this is what dying looks and feels like."

Eventually, both of Yu's legs were amputated below the hip, but she died the following year in spite of all the medical interventions. Mom said that Yu's tumors had spread and ate away her life.

Yu's doctor was a very tall and arrogant man full of attitude, with short, curly hair. His nose was out of proportion compared to the rest of his facial features, taking up two-thirds of his entire face. He walked funny, with his shoulders hunched forward, slouching, hips forward, and always one hand in his pocket. He liked to make jokes that no one found funny.

He made a joke about me once when I had just turned 13 and had my first period. I called my mom from a payphone at the rehab center and told her the news. My parents came the next day and drove me to a nearby store for some maxi pads. Even though my mom explained what to expect and what to do when I got my period, when it finally happened to me, I was nervous. But it wasn't just nervous, it was a sense of shame and guilt. It felt like I had done something wrong.

Are my friends going through this? Did they have their periods already? Feeling ashamed made sense though, in a cultural context. We were brought up thinking and believing that when a girl becomes a woman, we need to hide it from everyone else. We design our tampons to be smaller so we can fit them discreetly into our purse. We go to the drug store and come out with a bagful of groceries and make sure to tell the person bagging items to bury our feminine hygiene products at the bottom so no one will see them. We seek to hide the most natural thing that makes a woman a woman. We hide away because we feel the shame of people shaming us. So, when this doctor found out I was having my first period, he walked over to my bedside, where I was lying with closed eyes, pretending to be asleep. He said "Aww…

look at you, you are a woman now." And then he laughed. It wasn't *what* he said, but the *way* he said it that made me feel ashamed.

Chapter

Three

"'If only there could be an invention that bottled up a memory, like scent. And it never faded, and it never got stale. And then, when one wanted it, the bottle could be uncorked, and it would be like living the moment all over again.' I looked up at him, to see what he would say. He did not turn to me, he went on watching the road ahead."

— Daphne Du Maurier, *Rebecca*

My parents spent an enormous amount of time and energy supporting me through the healing process at the rehab center. Ever since I was admitted there, my dad's weekend excursions changed. Instead of driving 90 minutes to my grandparent's house, he now drove 90 minutes to visit me. Sometimes they would submit paperwork so I could spend the weekends at home; Dad would pick me up on Friday afternoon and drop me back Sunday night. It was almost like a boarding school, except I was there to fix my legs rather than receive an education.

By this time, all of my classmates had graduated from elementary school and were moving on to their first year in junior high school. When my accident happened, I was only in the fifth grade; I never made it to sixth grade, let alone graduation. When it was time for me to start junior high school, Dad had to pull some strings from his resources. Dad knew someone who knew the principle at my elementary school, and they worked out an arrangement to release an elementary diploma with my name on it so I could move on and apply for junior high school.

The rehab center also provided patients with an education from kindergarten through ninth grade, plus a vocational-skills school for anyone between the age of 16 to 18. Naturally, they placed me into the seventh grade when I was 13. My seventh-grade teacher, Mrs. Tsai, was this 60-year-old woman with straight white hair that hung to her shoulders. She had that typical look of an old Chinese lady that I'd seen many times on television, usually in programs depicting the Chinese Civil War era. Mrs. Tsai looked very assertive and serious, like she meant business.

One day I was late for class and she stopped me at the door and asked me why I was late. I explained that I was waiting to see my doctor to talk to him about scheduling my next surgery. She went on to tell me that I should never be late for class, and it was important for me to be on time for school. Sitting there in my wheelchair in front of my fellow students and teacher, I felt angry, so I raised my voice and yelled back at her.

"I am here to fix my legs, not to go to school! I did not come here for this and you can't tell me what I can or cannot do!"

She stood there silently and watched me turn red and hot, but didn't say a word to me after that and I didn't wait for her to respond. I turned my wheelchair around and rolled out.

A few days later, Mom and I ran into Mrs. Tsai at the parking lot. Mrs. Tsai and Mom started talking and I was there by their side. I looked into Mrs. Tsai's eyes and she smiled back at me while fully engaged in conversation with my mom. She told Mom I was a good student—that I learn fast and was very smart. She mentioned quite a number of positive things about me during her conversation, which made me feel guilty and ill at ease. I thought I was going to be in trouble, and that she was going to tell my mom how badly I behaved that day in front of the class. I thought she was going to rat me out and that I'd be punished for talking back to her. But she did none of that. Suddenly, I felt terrible. I felt ashamed. I felt bad for being mean to her.

Guilt can have such big influences on our own emotions, and in that moment during this brief encounter between my mom and Mrs. Tsai in the parking lot, millions of thoughts arose in my mind that replayed over and over in my head: "I wonder if she's going to tell Mom about what happened that day," "Is she going to say something bad about me?" and "What should I do? What do I say if mom ask me about it?" My mind was racing and plotting different scenarios of how this could go wrong even days after their conversation.

To my surprise, my teacher never brought up anything about what had happened. She never brought up the fact that I yelled at her in front of the class. She never mentioned a word about how badly I behaved.

Looking back, there were a few things I learned from that day and from my interaction with Mrs. Tsai at the rehab center. Today, whenever I find myself in a difficult situation, I think back to the way she handled that situation. She was calm and listened to what I had to say even though I lost my temper and talked back to her. She showed me what forgiveness could look like. No need to tell on someone, because within us we have the ability to reflect on things— including our own behavior. The shame and guilt that we all experience allows us to do just that; to self-reflect and course-correct, ultimately with the goal of becoming better people. It is also in those moments of guilt and shame that we catch a glimpse of who we truly are and who we are not.

Besides going to classes while living at the rehab center, I was also assigned to physical therapy. This took up a major portion of my day. Each child in rehab was assigned to a physical therapist, and before our sessions began, we would swim. There was an indoor swimming pool that everyone would climb into and move around in for an hour, followed by training with physical therapists at their workstations.

Through this physical therapy program, I learned how to swim. I swam so well that the director of physical therapy entered us in a swimming competition. The swim competition took place in the southern Taiwanese city of Kaohsiung. There was a total of five athletes in this competition, and I was in the youth group competition. My teammates were comprised of special athletes, and many of them would have the chance to compete on a national level, leading up to the Special Olympics competition. We were all physically challenged in some way; some of us had missing legs or missing arms, or limbs withered by polio and other ailments. The day before the competition, our swim coach bought train tickets for us, and together, we headed to the south by train.

I wore a red swimming suit that my mom bought me, goggles, and a swim hat. When my name was called, I got into the pool, put my goggles on, took a deep breath, and swam as fast as I could within my lane. I made a turn and kicked off with my feet against the wall of the swimming pool, giving me a head start compared to other athletes who couldn't use their feet when they turned. I came in first place in the youth group swimming competition and went home with a gold medal. This was the summer of 1988. This was the year they turned Tamsui Railroad—one of the oldest railroads built in Taipei—into history. In July 1988, Taipei Transit Official voted to abolish the railway line and convert it to MRT (Metro Rail Transit) line, bringing Tamsui, once a simple rural village, to prosperity. My teammates and I, along with our swim coach, took the Tamsui Railroad back to the rehab center.

After my initial accident, my doctor, Dr. Chiao, noticed that my bone composition and healing time was not optimal. Bone grew at a slower rate compared to other teenagers of the same age. Through the bone-healing process, Dr. Chiao also noticed my hip bones were not shaped properly. Dr. Chiao recommended inserting small plates and screws to stabilize those areas where the bones were most fragile and prone to deformities. It was decided that he would need to perform more operations on me to make those corrections.

The night before those surgeries, my dad would drop my mom off at the rehab center so she could spend nights with me, sleeping on a rollaway bed right next to mine in the patients' room. On those days, she would wake up early to leave the center and go to a nearby rental kitchen to cook for me. In Taiwan, we believe eating fish helps heal surgical wounds faster. Drinking soup made of pork ribs and Chinese herbs also makes our bodies stronger.

"I can't go to surgery for you, but I can make sure you have something to eat when you come out of there," Mom told me.

Before surgery, there was lots of preparation. I was told by nurses not to eat anything after six o'clock the night before. At seven o'clock at night, nurses would have to shave my legs and bowel-prep me with soap and water. Miss Cheng was the nicest among all the nurses who took care of me. This bowel-prep procedure can be very uncomfortable and embarrassing to a 13-year-old; Miss Cheng had to administer a gallon of soap and water to me rectally, and I would have to retain it for at least 15 minutes before I could go to the bathroom. Miss Cheng would talk to me through the whole process and her hands were always warmer than anybody else's.

On the day of the surgery, Mom watched me getting dressed in my surgical gown and hat, while nurses came to pick me up and push me on my gurney into the surgery room.

"You know the process already. Don't worry!" Mom said to me in a very encouraging way. "You'll be wide awake before you know it! See you soon, OK?"

In the surgery room, lying on the operating table with eyes wide open, I scanned the room looking at all the equipment and wondered what they were all used for.

"It is always cold inside the surgery room," I thought.

I gazed into the lights above me, feeling fascinated by them but also feeling a sense of anxiousness and nervousness. Then I threw up. It was not uncommon for me to experience side effects from the anesthesia drugs; subconsciously, the idea of going to surgery scared me so much that my default reaction was nausea and vomiting.

Through the reflection on the overhead surgical light, I saw someone standing up and walking towards me.

"Are you OK?" he asked.

"Yeah," I replied, lying on the table in my own vomit.

He cleaned me up, gave me a small tray, and told me that if I have to throw up again, to use it. I cried and I told him I didn't want to do this anymore. I didn't want to be operated on anymore and didn't want to feel sick every time. I was 13 years old, and "I don't want to" didn't seem to be an option for me. This was not a choice I had made. None of these were choices.

This is how it works: There are things that happen to us where we have to decide and make choices—often when we are given different options—and our decisions result in different possible outcomes. But then there are other things that are forced upon us in life that we have absolutely no control over. Sometimes, we aren't given the choice to decide between two or more possibilities; instead the choice is heaped upon us without our consent or permission. That was exactly what happened to me. I did not have a choice to be where I was. I did not get to choose between being hit by a car or having a normal day. I was forced by destiny and now here I am.

The man who handed me the small tray stood over me, holding up a mask, and told me he was going to let me sleep and rest a little bit. He asked me to count to 10. I began counting: one, two, three, four....

By the time I awoke, Dr. Chiao had finished placing metal plates on my hip bone, but it wouldn't be the last surgery for me. Many of the recovery nurses knew me well because I'd been coming in and out of surgery for years. They knew my name and my parents also bribed them with presents during holidays so they would take good care of me when my parents weren't around.

Many times I would sing for the nurses. One day, I turned and asked if I could sing. As egocentric as it sounds, I had a feeling that I was gifted. In Christianity, there are doctrines from the Bible that talk about angels, describing them as a heavenly order of beings, just below deities and above humanity. Although I come from a family rooted in Buddhism, I came across Christianity while living at the rehab center and I kind of liked the idea of angels. When there is nothing else for you to believe in times of tragedy, believing I might be gifted was the closest thing to heaven I could hope for. And you know what? Angels like to sing.

Each time I came out of surgery, I had a new scar on my legs, like a badge of honor. In a way it was like I got rewarded with a physical trophy to show the world I made it out alive that day. For a while, this actually became a hot collectable item among the children at the rehab center. There were competitions among us, comparing the number of "trophies" we collected on our bodies.

"How many do you have?"

"Thirteen," I counted.

"I only have 10." someone else said.

"Which one hurts more?" another person asked.

"This one, see how there are two holes? They put a device in to pull those bones apart."

These conversations happened often; everyone who was admitted either had some previous tragedy or was admitted because of genetic defects, and some had contracted polio in the 1970s. But no matter why the universe brought us there, we all shared the same experiences: those painful nights after surgery, the discriminatory looks and comments made from people when they noticed our physical differences. They called us "The Crippled."

It felt really nice to be able to belong somewhere. It's human nature to desire that sense of belonging. We thrive within a group even though many of us don't realize it. Albert Einstein said that "everything is made up of energy." Energy is the building block of all matter. The same energy that composes our bodies is the same that composes the bricks of the house you live in, your car, your phone, animals, and trees. It is all the same and that is all there is to it.

Energy is constantly flowing and changing form. It is everywhere and it can neither be created nor destroyed. Everything in this universe is made up of the same stuff. It is just present in different forms and shapes. But the universe is so big that each and every one of us is living on a different frequency and energy level. As a result, our radio can only be turned to one channel at a time. Every time we tap into the same energy, we feel connected. We feel safe. And we feel we belong.

It wasn't until many years later that I began to realize we are capable of tapping into a frequency that could allow us to have that same feeling of belonging within ourselves.

One of the world's most significant philosophers, Michel de Montaigne, once said that

"The greatest thing in this world is to know how to belong to oneself."

I was not the only person in my family affected by my personal tragedy. My sister, Emily, often spent her after-school hours traveling to visit me. Emily brought her sleeping blanket and pillow with her in the car. Mom always cut Emily's hair very short and, like other people who have older sister in the family, she wore a lot of my hand-me-down clothing including my favorite yellow polka-dot dress. She traveled with my parents to visit so often that she memorized her entire multiplication chart on those weekend trips to see me.

As for my brother, Mike was already in junior high school at the time I was admitted to the rehabilitation center. Oftentimes, I did not get to see him on weekends, since he went to after-school classes and usually stayed home alone while my parents came to visit me.

Looking back, I realize how my predicament inadvertently deprived my brother of his fair-share of access to my parents' love and attention all those years. After the accident, I became the center of everyone's focus, both mentally and physically. I became the center of my own tragedy, my own negative self-talk, and judgments. I convinced myself that all these unfortunate events happened to me and only me. I blamed others for showing their sympathy to me, but the truth was that I was feeling self-pity.

Living at the center gave me some comfort because this was the place where I was not being judged by what had happened, and more importantly, I was not caught up within my own tragedy. There were children much less fortunate than I was. And in a way, I felt glad. I felt glad that they weren't me. I will still have a chance to walk again. I sympathized with them and felt bad for them because many of them wouldn't be able to walk.

There were nights after my surgery when I sat on my bed crying. I held onto my legs, encased in plaster, surgical sites swollen inside the castm rubbing against the hard shell, pulsating, hot, and eager to come out. I elevated my legs on layers of pillow because I was told this would help ease the pain. Sitting up seemed to help with the excruciating pain. I looked around, and most of the time other patients would be asleep, but occasionally there would be someone sitting on the other side of the bed in my room doing the same thing. Our eyes would meet, and tears would fall down our faces while we rocked ourselves back and forth rhythmically, as if each forward motion was a scream out loud as we gave birth to our unconquerable souls.

Some nights were more painful than others, and I was told that taking too many painkillers was bad for you. When I first heard this from other children who have gone through surgeries, I took it into my heart and, as painful as it was after surgery, I resisted taking pain medications.

While I sat with my pain on those nights, my memories kept bringing me back to the school days when things were normal.

I thought about where I would have been right then. I could have been in junior high school along with all my other friends and we would have been studying hard by now to try and get ourselves into a better high school in a few years. I wanted to see all of my friends from school, I wanted to play jump rope with them in the schoolyard or play Hide and Seek with them by the tree in our schoolyard. I wanted to go back to the days before any of this had happened. I felt alone, hopeless, and shocked, but I was still just a kid who wanted to be like her friends.

There is a very specific kind of prison many of us endure—one in which we keep ourselves locked in and continue to live through it because we are too afraid to be kind to ourselves and allow those memories holding us back to pass through so we can move on. We repeat to ourselves what *should* have happened, what *could* have been done, and what *would* have worked. The stories replay in our minds like a recording.

What we don't realize is that there is a natural process that occurs everywhere, to everything we see, feel, and touch around us. Life is a cycle of changes. Unhappiness arises when we resist those changes, because it is natural to flow in a state of constant movement. Creating barriers to this flow leads to destructive flooding and overwhelming chaos, whereas accepting those changes can lead to balance, harmony, and abundance. A caterpillar morphing into a butterfly cannot un-butterfly itself through resistance.

For the most part, I am an optimist. Looking around me, everyone I knew was going through the same difficult, painful time. Everyone was either born with some kind of disability or some tragedy had befallen them. I felt fortunate that I was not them but, in a way, I *was* them.

One day, my mom was talking to another mom whose daughter—who experienced some kind of nerve damage when she was little—also lived at the center. I overheard the adults' conversation. The other mom commented on how good I was for being optimistic regardless of what had happened to me. I looked over at my mom and my mom replied proudly and agreed with the other mom. She said she was glad that I didn't look down on myself and that I was naturally optimistic and strong. She said that she was glad that I was not resentful of what had happened and that I never blamed her for my current situation.

For many years, I was living up to that expectation; not looking down on myself, being optimistic, and being strong. Every word in that conversation stayed with me as I did not want to disappoint my mom or anyone else. I learned to move around when both of my legs were in the plaster cast, lifting them up and using my upper body strength to move from the wheelchair up onto the bed and vice versa. I stopped asking for help as long as I was capable, and if something was entirely out of my reach, I learned to come up with an alternative. I did not want people to believe that I was weak. I stopped crying in front of people, I held my head high, and my ego higher. But deep down inside, I felt small, and like a hypocrite when it came to being optimistic, since I definitely did not feel strong. I didn't want people to know that about myself, not even my mom. For many years, the only safe place to let go of my emotions was my own closet.

Chapter

Four

"And the danger is that in this move toward new horizons and far directions, that I may lose what I have now, and not find anything except loneliness."

— Sylvia Plath, *The Unabridged Journals of Sylvia Plath*

By the time I was 14 and had been living in the rehab center for three years, I was finally able to go home. At the same time, my family received letters from United States immigration saying that our application for residency had been granted. We were getting ready to move to America.

I was given a pair of metal leg braces which added about a pound of weight to my legs, and also a pair of arm crutches to help me get around. Dr. Chiao said I would need to wear these until I turned 18 to prevent any deformities from occurring as I grew. The leg braces came with a pair of ugly open-toe shoes that didn't really match with any outfit I wore. Over time, I learned to walk to school in them.

I was 15 by the time I went back to junior high school. I was no longer in the same class as all my other friends; instead, I had to start from the very beginning of seventh grade, which meant being in a new class of students with new teachers. I was still the shortest person in the class, so once again I was placed on the first row in my class.

"Do you have polio?" some kids at school would ask me.

"No! I don't have polio," I replied.

"Why are you wearing that? It must be polio."

"I *told* you I don't have polio," I repeated angrily.

Many of my new classmates didn't know about my accident four years earlier, and when they saw me wearing those chunky metal leg braces, they assumed it was polio. For the most part, they were really nice to me. I never had to go to my physical education class, and never played volleyball or any other sports with them. In the morning, we had a routine of gathering together out on the field and raising our flags and singing the national anthem together. I never had to be part of that either. Anything and everything that involved physical activity, I was excused from having to participate in. For a while it felt normal to be absent from these gatherings, and from sports or anything else that required physical strength, but I began to feel left out and alone. I felt I was being left behind, and because of that, I was bitter.

One day, a classmate and I were talking. He had an injury of some kind and was excused from going to the morning ceremony. We were the only two students left in the classroom. I made a comment about how my parents and I were going to America. How life was going to be so much better there. He commented that America is not that much better, and that I was betraying my own country and should feel bad about it.

I was upset and bitter. Instead of accepting his opinion for what it was, I jumped up and attacked him with harsh words. We ended up fighting before the rest of the class returned and I stopped talking to him. I never apologized to him after our fight. He attempted to open up to me to restart a conversation, but I was way too proud to step into forgiveness and allow him or anyone else to come into my life. Later, he must have written something in the weekly review assignments we were all required to turn in. My teacher, Mr. Lee, was a 32-year-old newly graduated chemistry teacher. He wrote to me in red marker about my perspectives and how he felt there was a need for me to resolve this with my classmate.

He said, "Going to America is great, but until you can learn to appreciate where you are *now*, you will never be able to find contentment in life." His words were sharp like a knife, forcing me to reflect on my own flaws. My pride was punched and I felt ashamed for what I had said and how I felt. It was like an invisible slap to the face, putting me into my place.

There's a belief that when the universe closes a door on you, another one will open. I am a firm believer in that. There've been signs along the way since my injury that speak to this belief. There were people who kept showing up at my door and teaching me valuable lessons in life at the right moment in the right place and time.

Mr. Lee had a strong personality; he was assertive, determined, and full of energy. He had short hair, slightly slouching shoulders, and always seemed to be cold. He often wore a burgundy jacket, and always showed up to our class looking angry about something or someone. He was strict but taught us well.

During lunchtime, he would bring his lunch box and eat with us in the class. He would set up his desk and lunch right in front of the class, and most of the time, his desk faced mine. There he would be, looking straight at me and my lunch box. He finished everything in his lunch box, with not a single crumb of leftover food. He glanced over at me and saw me eating, scrunching his eyebrows and giving me a look.

"Are you going to finish that?" he seemed to be saying with his expression.

"You need to finish that before I preach to you about wasting food."

"Do you know how much effort your mom put into making that for you?"

My thoughts were working like a runaway train.

All those silent phrases popping into my head, even though it was just a look on his face. Guilt works in funny ways. It's all in our heads, and doesn't even require others to take any action and yet we start these thought-trains that drive us nuts.

That day, instead of closing my lunch box and leaving all the leftovers to take home with me, I finished everything, not wasting a bite. What I've also learned from that day was how not to waste food. Eat what is on your plate and never take more than you can finish.

During the first semester of seventh grade, the school was undergoing some remodeling. Our classroom shifted around from time to time, and sometimes we didn't have a classroom at all. Instead, we'd have classes in one section of the hallway; tables and chairs and a black board. Occasionally I could see across from our hallway to the other side of the school yard where my friends were. They were in the ninth grade already and getting ready to take the national examination to move on to high school. This was back in the era when Taiwan's school system was still based heavily on examinations and placements. I wondered what it would be like to be in that class and wished I could be a part of it.

Sometimes, I think that the idea that "the grass is always greener on the other side" is rooted in jealousy and envy, and could even lead to depression. I've always wondered what life would be like had I not missed out on those three years of my life. Who would my best friend be by now? Which class would I be in? But things didn't work out that way.

In Taiwan, there were regulations dictating that boys under 18 were forbidden to travel outside of the country until they served their duty in the military. Mike was already 17 by the time our immigration papers came through. On July 19, 1989, before I got to the second semester in seventh grade, my family was ready to emigrate to the United States. We sold our house and left our friends and family in Taiwan. Mike moved in with my uncles and aunts who were still living at the veteran village, while the four of us—my parents, Emily, and I—packed our bags and prepared to move to the other side of the world.

Our flight was not a direct flight. We had a layover in Tokyo for a few hours prior to our connecting flight to New York. None of us spoke any English. My sister took some classes when we were still in Taiwan and learned how to say "hamburger" and "water." Other common words we already knew were "please,""thank you," and "you're welcome." I learned some English in school, too, learning to say, "this is a book," "that is a desk," "good morning," "good afternoon,"and "good evening."

When we deplaned in Tokyo, my mom took my sister for a walk through the airport. They came back with a can of Coca-Cola. As my sister started drinking it, Mom remarked that it was expensive. "It was $5— that's 200 NT dollars if you do the conversion." Of course, my sister did not care, and was having a blast and enjoying her soda. This was our lives for the first few years, converting all the currency and comparing US dollars to New Taiwanese dollars to get a sense of the value for anything we purchased.

We waited at the gate for our connecting flight to New York. Most of our belongings—things like books and clothing—we shipped to America. What we had with us were simple necessities, like clothing for immediate use. I also carried the guitar I inherited from my brother. A man sitting across from me looked at my guitar, a Spanish make with nylon strings, and a dark burgundy neck and body that I had plastered with stickers. The man pointed to the guitar and asked me if he could play it. I nodded.

He picked up the guitar and started playing. It was a song I'd never heard before. The melody reminded me of songs we sang at church. They consisted of happy notes— notes that make up a G major chord. Songs like "Blackbird" by the Beatles; "Brown Eyed Girl" by Van Morrison; even "Frosty the Snowman" by Willie Nelson. I don't recall what song he played but he played it really well. There was a sense of joy and happiness behind the tune. He handed the guitar back to me and pointed to it again. I reckon he was probably asking if it was mine. I nodded again.

There's a human connection in every encounter we have with other people we meet in our lives. Sometimes a complete stranger shows up at our doorstep, and while we may not speak the language, nor look the same, nor share the same path, in the midst of our busy lives, we connect. There are many ways to connect with each other in this world; through words, through music, through body language, through our feelings and emotions, and through listening to each other.

We are more together than alone in many ways. It was my first time meeting a complete non-Asian, English-speaking human being, yet I felt safe and connected through the melody he played.

Chapter

Five

"I hate to hear you talk about all women as if they were fine ladies instead of rational creatures. None of us want to be in calm waters all our lives."

— Jane Austen, *Persuasion*

efore moving to the United States, my dad taught military course work at a high school in Taiwan. As far as I could remember, Dad had always had an office job, sitting behind a desk and handling paperwork, grading exams, and writing speeches for me back in my elementary school days. When we first arrived in America, we could barely afford KFC. Dad found a job at a Chinese supermarket where he didn't have to speak much

English and language wouldn't be a barrier. His job involved lifting heavy crates when shipments arrived. The job paid very little and offered no health insurance. On his first day of work, he came home with cuts and bruises on his hands. Those were the hands that once held delicate pens and paper, not brutish crates of vegetables and heavy bottles.

I was 15 by the time we settled in New York, and I already started to have a sense that life in America was going to be tough. We didn't know anybody besides my uncle's family and my grandparents who were living in New York at the time. This was to be a whole new life we were starting, and it involved the entire family. Seeing the cuts and bruises on my dad's hands that first day he came home from work rattled something inside of me, making me feel sad and resentful.

"Why did we have to come here?" I wondered to myself. "No one here cares about us."

It seemed as if everyone had their own lives to worry about, and even though we were renting a room from my uncle Leo and living under the same roof, I had a feeling that he and Aunt Carol weren't very empathetic toward us. Mom and Uncle Leo made an agreement that she would work for Uncle Leo at the beauty salon he owned in Queens, New York.

Every night, Emily and I would walk 15 blocks to meet Mom and walk her back home another 15 blocks while Dad stayed home and cooked. After we received our green cards, Dad went back to Taiwan to take care of my brother, and only returned to the United States every six months to maintain his resident status. Our family was divided into two during the first three years in America, and things were very different from how they were in Taiwan. I was the second-oldest child in the family and there was a sense of responsibility that fell upon my shoulders, while simultaneously, I was coping with my own awkward teenage period.

With the help of my Aunt Susie, my mom and I went to the local public school for enrollment. I was wearing my leg braces when we arrived at the school administration office, and as I walked into the room, a lady who was helping us at the counter told my mom that I needed to be in a special education class. My mom didn't speak English, but Aunt Susie explained to my mom what "special education" meant, and my mom was livid at the lady from the admin office. Mom fought for me, saying I didn't belong in special education. She insisted the lady at the admin office hand us the application, and enrolled me in the public school system.

My parents also enrolled Emily and me into an after-school program to learn English and help us with our homework. Emily and I took the bus to the tutoring center, and while the tutor was supposed to teach us English and help us do our homework, instead, we were handed a dictionary and told to look up the words ourselves. It was math homework I was working on that day, and even though it was simple algebra that I had already learned in Taiwan, in order for me to understand the problem, I had to look up every single word in the equation, translate it into Chinese, *then* solve the math problem.

It felt discouraging, as if my life was at a standstill. I was looking up every word in the dictionary and learning everything from scratch. It wasn't affecting my sister as much as it was me. Emily was 10 years old at the time and always had a more optimistic personality than I did. The sense of responsibility and the feeling of being stranded in a foreign country with no friends weighed down on me, and on top of all that, I was wearing chunky metal leg braces and arm crutches. Everywhere I went, it felt strange, isolating, and wrong.

Despite all the obstacles I was facing at the age of 15, there was one thing Emily and I really looked forward to on our walks to pick up Mom: stopping at KFC. We still didn't speak much English, and the first time we tried to order, we failed miserably. We didn't know how it worked, let alone the differences between dark meat or thighs or drumsticks. One evening we walked in and, as we stood in line to order, tried working it out in advance, talking between ourselves in Chinese and doing a little prep talk before ordering. The lady behind the counter happened to speak Chinese, and she jumped in and started conversing with us in our native language, really taking her time to help us. From then on, it was always a relief to see the Chinese lady working the night shift, knowing she would help us order our food.

Having a language barrier diminished my

confidence when it came to speaking and writing. I learned to process words in my head in Chinese, translate them into English, and reconstruct the word sequence before speaking out loud. Some say learning a new language is like grasping at straws; you try to make sense out of a string of sounds coming at you, translate that string of sounds in your head, and hope you understood correctly, together with the person's body language. Just thinking about this whole mental process of translating each word is exhausting!

I don't remember exactly when this mental processing of words suddenly disappeared, but it did. Life sometimes happens this way, too. We find ourselves in uncomfortable situations and try to make sense of everything coming toward us. It felt like I was drowning, hopelessly grabbing on to any floating object I could see, hoping to be saved.

Things became easier and easier with both reading and speaking. Through the struggle of learning a new language, I discovered that the only way to save myself from drowning was through change. It took time, commitment, and courage to challenge myself over and over again. By the time I was in my junior year of high school, I fought my way from ESL class to a regular English class. Change was uncomfortable. Change was inevitable. Change was also what I needed to move forward.

While my dad went back to Taiwan to look after my brother, my mom worked at my uncle's beauty salon in Queens. We also rented a bedroom from my uncle in the home where he and his family lived. It was my mom, my sister, and me, all sleeping together in a room that was less than 100 square feet. This room fit a queen-size bed, a full-size bed placed perpendicular to the other, and a temporary closet made of vinyl where we kept all of our belongings. We shared the living area and kitchen with my uncle and his family. The only things we owned at the time were our clothes and a secondhand desk where my sister and I did our homework. We didn't have a car, telephone, television, or anything else you might consider a luxury.

At night, when Emily and I wanted to watch TV, we had to ask for permission to watch it in Uncle Leo and Aunt Carol's bedroom. Many times, my six-year-old cousin, Harry, would decide what we watched. Finally, after a year, right around Thanksgiving when everything was on sale, Uncle Leo bought us a 20-inch TV. It felt good and powerful to no longer have to accommodate anyone else's preferences when it came to watching TV. We had a remote control and we felt powerful.

After school, my sister and I stayed home watching TV and doing our homework. Sometimes Harry would join us, but he usually ended up going to my maternal grandparents' house and they would watch him. My grandparents were typical Chinese who valued and favored boys over girls, and smarter kids over average kids. Hence, while my mom was growing up, she was never treated as if she was someone special. But what I learned from my mom was that she had a lot of compassion toward others.

Even though she was not the favorite in the house, she was the one who ended up taking care of both of my grandparents in their last few years of life. She was there for them, even at their deathbeds.

When I was little, Mom would sit us around the cassette player and play us recordings that my grandparents sent to her from the United States. Communicating by telephone was expensive back then, so people sent cassette recordings to each other as a way of communicating through voice and sound. Sometimes Mom would replay these cassettes over and over again. Most of the time, it was just my grandmother talking about their new lives in the United States. Sometimes my aunt Shelly and my grandfather would take over the speaking, and it often sounded like they were just sitting in the same room having a casual conversation with my mom.

If I learned anything from my mom, it is that to give is really all there is to life. You may not always get what you give, but that should not stop you from giving. She never stops giving to her family.

Because of our financial situation, my family couldn't afford to enroll me in a physical therapy program in the United States. Instead, I managed to walk and figure things out on my own. Since I was the oldest in the house at the time and Mom had to work every day until seven o'clock at night, I had to take on many chores in the house. I would go to the market around the corner of our apartment building or to the Chinese supermarket to pick up produce and gallons of milk. When I got home from school, I would make dinner for my sister and me while waiting until it was time to pick up my mom from the beauty salon. I was really good at making stir-fried beef with onion, stir-fried celery with pork, and stir-fried egg and tomato, not because I liked them, but because they were the only dishes I knew how to cook.

There were nights I'd turn to the side of my bed, only to wake up seeing tiny cockroaches crawling on the wall. Other nights I found myself sobbing silently, trying not to wake my mom or my sister. I wanted to go back home in Taiwan, but I knew that this was our home now—100 square feet with a television that was given to us as a gift. This was all we had. It was on those nights that I made a promise to myself. "I am going to be better, even though I don't know what 'better' means." This idea of needing to be better became more pronounced as I reached my sixteenth birthday.

My sister and I were at my grandparents' place after school one day playing with my cousin. Suddenly, he began hitting my sister with the toy in his hand. I stopped him, yelling "No!" He cried, capturing the attention of my grandfather, who gave me a look but didn't say anything. After we got home, I received a phone call from Aunt Shelly.

"You should not be mean to your cousin!"Aunt Shelly said.

"I wasn't," I insisted. "He was hitting my sister."

"You are living in their house; you need to be grateful!"she continued.

"What are you talking about? What does this have to do with him hitting my sister?"

"You are a devil!," she shouted. "You are a disgrace to your family! You should learn how to be thankful when people offer you a place to live. Uncle Leo and Aunt Carol pay your grandparents $20 a month to look after your cousin. How much are you guys paying them to watch you and your sister?"

It was in that moment that I realized it wasn't about who was misbehaving; it was about who was paying more. It was about being rich versus being poor. It was about how much we can or cannot pay to receive the same treatment that we deserved from our own beloved grandparents. It was a heartbreaking lesson to learn from my own family members.

"You are a demon!" Aunt Shelly shouted at me.

Those words echoed in my ears after I hung up the phone with her. I felt hopeless and hurt. My family was poor, but the reason we were poor was because we left everything that was familiar and came to America, a place where dreams could come true. I cried as I left the apartment and began walking. I walked a block to my friend's house and told her what had happened. We cried together but at the end of my cry, I knew I needed to be better. I got up, dried my tears, and went home.

"I need to be better." I told myself.

At night, I told my mom what Aunt Shelly said, and Mom called her to talk about how inappropriate it was for her to call me a demon and speak to me that way. Mom stood up for me, even though it was

Aunt Shelly who had applied for immigration on our behalf.

That night, the three of us had a discussion in the tiny bedroom with the big TV. I told my sister that someday, when I grew up, I would make lots of money, and I would ask for that money in the form of coins, which I will throw at Aunt Shelly. It would be her payback day! My sister and I both laughed hard till we fell asleep.

Do people look at you differently when you have more wealth? Of course they do. They treat you *nicer*. We live in a society where personal values are equated with dollar signs. The idea that "money can buy you anything" has been passed down through generations. Do people say different things to you when you are highly educated? Of course, they do. Depending on the way you use your vocabulary, people may assume you are better educated, or make assumptions about your social status. Do people look at you through a different lens when you look different? Of course, they do. They want to know what is special about you.

We live in a world full of judgments. Not only do we judge ourselves, but we also judge other people and the things around us. We judge based on "the standard," "the norm," what's "typical," and "the usual." These judgments were introduced to us early in our own childhoods and became fully developed in adulthood. These are the limiting beliefs and assumptions we have been taught that have been passed on from generation to generation.

Judgments are part of our culture, part of our roots, and also part of who we *believe* we are. These are our viewpoints and understanding of how the world *should* be. We have been conditioned to believe that these beliefs and assumptions speak about truth. What is being said by many must be true, right?

No—not everything you hear or see is *The Truth*.

Perhaps one day, in your own experience, the things you believed to be true will become the reasons you feel stuck in life. Maybe you believed that a woman can't take on a role in leadership because your great grandmother was not a leader and therefore = "women cannot become leaders" was part of your thought pattern. Perhaps you believe eating a lot of carbohydrates will make you gain weight, so you avoid consuming them and thus deprive yourself of eating bread, pasta, and other foods you enjoy. Regardless of what beliefs you have been conditioned to hold true, clinging to those beliefs may be the reason you feel stuck.

How true is it that you need to have a lot of money in order for someone to treat you well? How true is it that you have to have a higher education in order to speak eloquently? And how true is it that you need to look a certain way in order to be special?

Bringing awareness to our own belief systems is a lot like culture shock to many people as they see, hear, and touch things and ideas that are completely different from what they were raised believing to be true. It challenges our beliefs and it releases our judgments of ourselves and others.

It is not until we are able to see the essence of who we truly are that we can begin to tell the difference between what is true versus what is *The Truth.*

It wasn't Aunt Shelly's fault that she valued wealth more than family. It was through her own experiences, her own limiting beliefs and assumptions that she learned to value material things over anything else. The people who stared at me and took a hard look at my physical differences or asked, "What is wrong with you?"were not saying anything about who *I* am, but rather about who *they* are and the beliefs they have carried with them. I was, indeed, different, and many had never seen anyone physically different from themselves. It also wasn't my fault that I would compare myself to other women when our society places so much emphasis on physical appearance.

I was taught to see my body in a certain way based on our social conditioning: a woman should be at least five foot two, be slender, have fully developed breasts, her glutes should be tight, she should have long hair, and wear fitted and flattering dresses.

And this was the image of a woman I believed to be real.

Chapter
Six

"You need to learn how to select your thoughts just the same way you select your clothes every day. This is a power you can cultivate."

— Elizabeth Gilbert, *Eat, Pray, Love*

In the morning, Emily and I would walk to the bus stop and take public transportation to school. The bus that ran on Main Street dropped me off right in front of my high school. Emily's school was closer than mine and she would usually get off the bus before I did. Every day as I walked to the bus stop, there was a nice lady who worked on the second floor above the supermarket who would say hi to me. I was comfortable saying hi to her, but we never engaged in conversation because I didn't yet have the confidence to strike up a conversation with a stranger with my elementary-level English. At school, I'd see clusters of students hanging around with others who spoke their native tongues. As immigrants facing so many challenges in our new country, it was more comfortable for s-and far less scary-to communicate in the languages we already knew.

A sense of belonging is something we all look for in our lives. Oftentimes we feel more comfortable around groups who share similar life experiences. Whether it's the language we speak, the color of our skin, the religious group we belong to, or the last name you have in common. We search for those commonalities to create bonds and a sense of connectedness. This is why we look for community, groups, and tribes whenever we find ourselves alone. Human beings were not designed to be isolated; we were designed to be together.

Even after being discharged from the rehabilitation center, I was still not fully recovered; my left leg was shorter than the right leg by 2.5 cm, so my leg braces were designed to compensate for that difference. When I wasn't wearing the leg braces, friends would make fun of me, calling me a penguin, because that's exactly how I walked. I'd take short steps while waddling around from side to side with my ponytail swinging in the back of my head. People watched and kids made fun of me as I made my way down the block toward the bus stop.

To compensate for the shorter left leg, all my shoes were custom made. For every new pair of shoes

I would buy, I would have to find a cobbler to add 2.5 cm to the sole of my left shoe.

During my awkward teenage years, I had very limited choices when it came to shoes. I wanted to look prettier and more normal, so I decided to put away the ugly leg brace—a big piece of rubber glued to the bottom of regular shoes with metal frames that ran all the way up to my thigh—that the doctors told me to wear until I was 18. And even though that 2.5 cm doesn't look drastically bad on a ruler, when you're wearing a shoe with a thick piece of rubber attached to the bottom, it doesn't look very pretty at all. I wanted to be seen as a "normal," which meant getting rid of that metal shoe, putting away my crutches, and walking like an able-bodied person.

For me, the word "normal" is defined by my own physical appearance as it relates to others. My idea of a "normal" person comes from all the images I've seen in textbooks, on social media, and even through observing human anatomy in the general population. The average height for adult women varies around the world. In the United States, it is a little under five feet four inches tall. When I think about "normal," I compare myself to someone who falls into the average-height category. I am a four foot, four inch grown adult woman.

When I think about being "normal," I compare myself to the average body shape of all women, historically described in categories such as "triangle," "rectangle," "diamond," "oval," and "hourglass." For many years, I couldn't look at a photo of my own body because I don't quite fit under the average "normal" body shape.

But what is normal for one person can mean something different to another. How we interpret the word depends on our experiences and personal circumstances. Until we have learned to let go of the judgments we impose on ourselves and others, the word "normal" and its synonyms "average," "common," and "typical" will always be associated with emotional triggers.

In school I was not very noticeable and was not someone who stood out from the crowd. I tried to blend in as much as possible despite my height and waddling walk. My parents discovered my artistic skills at a very young age, and sent me to art school and let me take piano lessons. When the school started a Chinese magazine club, I got involved in the club because of my artistic talent. I was also good at writing and had a way with words, and my Chinese teacher, Mr. Yao, took notice of my talent. I would often write short essays as part of the assignments that received the highest grades in the class. It felt good knowing I was good at something. I was going through the stages of identifying myself and discovering who I was around the ages of 16 and 17.

During high school, while holding the Editor's position for the Chinese magazine, I met Ben, a boy from my Chinese class. He was from Malaysia, very talented, and good looking too; tall, handsome, and shy at times. He was good at illustration and sometimes before class Ben would take out a piece of paper and draw cartoons. I thought it was amazing and really admired him for his talent. I liked him a lot.

One day, I decided I was going to write Ben a letter—a love letter. It was going to express my feelings for him because I was too shy and insecure to tell him directly. I wrote the letter with all of my heart and expressed how I felt about him. I brought it to class the next day and handed it to him, watching his reaction. He was polite, but didn't read it while we faced each other. I went on to my classes that day and when I came back to the classroom, as I moved toward the garbage can to throw something away, there it was: the letter I had written to him, the beautiful stationary scrunched up inside the basket. My heart broke and there was a little voice that came into my mind that said, "Of course he doesn't like you. Why would he?"

It was the first time I discovered that particular voice in my head; the voice that has always been there whispering things to me after the accident. But what was different about the voice this time was that it wasn't whispering anymore; it was louder than usual—so loud that I could not ignore it much longer, so I started listening to it every time it spoke.

A few months later, I found out that Ben was seeing another girl, Linda, from our class. Linda was much prettier, taller, and thinner than I was, very stylish, and physically normal. She epitomized the average teenage girl: five feet two inches tall, mid-length hair, slender, soft spoken, and an hourglass-shaped body.

And the voice in my head was speaking again to me: "Of course they would be together. Ben is handsome and Linda is pretty. They look better together than he and I would have looked."

Seeing them together made me felt very conscious about my own body. I began wearing long pants instead of shorts, and baggy clothes and t-shirts that sat below my waist, making me look even shorter and more out of proportion. On a hot summer's day, when everyone stripped away their long winter coats and snow boots, I put on my stockings and shirt to cover all the scars on my legs.

I didn't have a lot of confidence in how I looked, and this definitely become more apparent in the way I dressed myself. I had a lot of oversized t-shirts and jeans, and I rarely wore skirts to school. When I started seeing other girls at school wearing heels and pretty dresses, I felt jealous toward them.

"I wish I could wear that." I thought to myself.

Besides being more conscious about my looks, I also began caring more about the way others were treating me, and related how they treated me to the way I looked.

One day after school, I got on the bus like I normally would, and the bus was packed with students heading home. All the seats were taken so I was forced to stand and find a place to hold on. Finally, I found a spot and held onto the side of a seat. The bus started moving and soon after, the girl sitting in that seat pushed my hand away. She gave me a look that said she didn't want me to stand next to her or hold onto the seat handle. I was embarrassed. I didn't know what to do and didn't speak much English, so I felt especially hopeless and unable to defend myself. I ended up moving toward the front of the bus and holding onto the side of someone else's seat.

Even though I didn't feel pretty enough, there were certain things I knew I was good at. I was in ESL class for a very long time, but I was always on top of my homework, making sure I did all the assignments on time and keeping up with my English studies. One of my ESL teachers, Ms. Kaplain, noticed my talent and nominated me for a community speech contest among ESL students within the region. I was given a poem to recite for the competition.

"*Invictus* by Ernest Henley."
I recited in front of the audience.

Out of the night that covers me,
Black as the pit from pole to pole,
I thank whatever gods may be
For my unconquerable soul.

In the fell clutch of circumstance
I have not winced nor cried aloud.
Under the bludgeoning of chance
My head is bloody, but unbowed.

Beyond this place of wrath and tears
Looms but the Horror of the shade,
And yet the menace of the years
Finds and shall find me unafraid.

It matters not how strait the gate,
How charged with punishments the scroll,
I am the master of my fate,
I am the captain of my soul."

I remember reciting this poem word for word, just how Ms. Kaplain and I had practiced in school. I did not understand why she came up with this poem for me to recite, but we spent hours after school where she would have me stand in front of her and recite it to her. She was taller than the average American woman with big bones and dark brunette shoulder-length hair. She always wore a white blouse with a long A-line skirt. Ms. Kaplain was in her late fifties and had a very assertive look on her face when she taught our class. Every time we practiced, she would correct my pronunciation, one word at a time.

During our practice, Ms. Kaplain wanted me to give the poem meaning, to feel the poetry, to own the meaning behind those words and express them as if they were part of me. I flipped open the cover of the paper folder she handed to me and there was the entire poem in front of me. First, I read through it several times to translate words in my head. Then I read through it out loud to hear how it sounded. When I reached the part that said "I am the master of my fate; I am the captain of my soul," I did not really understand what the words meant, and wasn't yet able to reflect upon them and make them sound more meaningful and more personal to me.

The way I saw myself was how short I was

compared to my peers. I walked funny, and as I grew older, my legs began to show signs of deformity; they looked crooked. The more I noticed them, the more I felt ashamed about my own body and the more I wanted to hide.

When people made comments to me like, "You are beautiful," "You are smart," or "You are brave," deep down inside I didn't believe them.

I imprisoned myself in an endless circle of negative beliefs. Some of those beliefs were about how an average woman should look and behave— ideas passed down to me through generations. I had no sense of self-identity because I didn't have what I needed to fit the social norms or standards.

As I recited the poem, words crept beneath that shield of bone and flesh, and I felt there was something different about me. Words moved me but I didn't completely understand them. I had a sense of who I was, I knew I had a spirit and a soul, and that perhaps there was something deeper and more meaningful inside of me.

By the time my dad and brother had moved back to the United States to join the rest of the family, we needed to move out of Uncle Leo's place and get a home of our own. We had money from selling our house in Taiwan, and my parents also borrowed money from our relatives and friends to help pay for a house. But still, we had very limited financial resources, so we ended up taking out a mortgage and purchasing a two-family home in Queens, together with my uncle's family. They occupied the second floor and we lived on the first floor. My dad took over my grandfather's business making sweet rice pudding—old-fashioned Chinese pudding made with fermented sweet rice that contains low levels of alcohol. This traditional food is believed to have many benefits, including lowering cholesterol and supporting overall health. According to Chinese literature, the pudding is also good for postpartum women and during the menstruation cycle to keep the body warm.

After school, we didn't do a lot of extracurricular activities because the sweet rice pudding business required a lot of manpower, and it was virtually impossible for my dad to do it all by himself. It was not uncommon for my brother, my sister, and me to rotate shifts to help prepare these puddings. My mom was still working as a hair stylist at my uncle's salon, and now that we lived further away, she would take the bus to and from work. Many times, she wouldn't get home till after eight at night. I picked up the cooking responsibilities during these periods when neither of my parents were available to make dinner for us.

Mom and Dad would go grocery shopping on weekends, and I would end up making dinner for everyone to make sure we had food on the table by the time Mom got home. It turned out I enjoyed cooking and coming up with new ideas for dinner. I tried out different recipes and learned how to cook on my own. The biggest challenges I faced, though, was that everything in the kitchen was up high, and

I was short. The stovetop was really tall, and all the cabinets were hard to reach for someone as short as I was. Because of my physical limitations, I began learning tricks for overcoming these unavoidable challenges. I asked my dad to make a small step-stool, which I positioned right in front of the stove so I wouldn't have to keep raising my arms when I reached for the wok. I would also pull a chair next to me, so that when I needed plates and bowls, I could climb up the chair and use that as a ladder to get to those hard-to-reach places.

Thinking back to those days, it's no wonder I have such a strong upper body today. All that lifting, climbing, and pulling heavy objects helped strengthen my muscles.

Our new home consisted of three bedrooms, a bathroom, and a basement, which Dad ended up using as his workspace. We set up rooms where the fermented rice puddings would be stored and processed. The money we had after borrowing and selling our house in Taiwan left us a little bit extra to put a downpayment on a minivan. We were all excited about having a car because we'd been using public transportation for the first five years of our lives in the United States. Owning a car meant we could travel further and do more things, including delivering the sweet rice pudding to markets and wholesalers in Brooklyn. But the biggest benefit of having a car in the family meant that I no longer needed to use public transportation to get to school.

For the last two years of high school, Dad would

wait for me after school and drive me home. I didn't have to wait for the crowded bus and worry about having a place to sit, and most importantly, I didn't have to feel bad about myself because of how other kids at the school looked at me when I got on the bus. I was suddenly free of being judged by them. I didn't have to be noticed by anybody. This was important to me because I hated to see the looks on people's faces when they saw me; those pitying, "I feel sorry for you" looks, and the "why are you so short?" kind of messages they sent me from across the room.

I recognized my ability to pick up on these emotions from people really early on in my life. Sometimes, my family would joke about something and I would be extremely sensitive to what they said, how they said it, and what they meant by it. I have learned from my own family that I am probably the most sensitive child in the family. I cried a lot, I got angry a lot, I was very stubborn, and I got frustrated when things didn't turn out the way I wanted them to. It wasn't until much later that I learned the term "empath" and how it applied to me.

Many times, I believed that being an empath was a gift, but also a curse. After the accident, it was as if a switch was flipped and suddenly, I began to not only feel a lot of self-judgment toward myself, but I also developed the ability to empathize deeply with others—to feel what they feel. I understood what it meant to have painful nights and experience some of life's most unbearable challenges. When others around me were feeling this way, I could feel it too.

As for the bus ride, I no longer needed to take all that in. I no longer needed to concern myself with other people's perceptions of me—at least for that short period of time riding home.

Chapter

Seven

"To the outside world, we all grow old. But not to brothers and sisters. We know each other as we always were. we know each other's hearts. we share private family jokes. We remember family feuds and secrets, family griefs and joys."

— Clara Ortega, as cited in
Chicken Soup for the Sister's Soul 2

E ver since moving into the new house, Emily and I shared a room together. We took over the master bedroom because we needed to fit our writing desks *and* out beds in there. Mom and Dad got us bunk beds and, because of my disability, Emily ended up with the top bunk. Growing up, Emily and I were closer to each other than I was with Mike. My mom wanted another child after I was born, and before she had my sister, my mom was pregnant with another child, but it never made it into the world. A few years later, Emily was born.

"It would have been nice if we had another boy," my mom said. But as it turned out, a sister was what *I* needed. Someone to keep me company and someone I could boss around while immobilized after the accident. But I do agree with my mom that having another boy would have been nice for my brother Mike.

I felt guilty for not being very close to Mike, especially considering he was the only boy in our family and had a sister like me who took a lot of our parents' attention. While we were growing up, Mike always played alone and went through those awkward teenage years by himself while Mom and Dad were busy taking care of me at the hospital.

Before we moved to the United States when I was 15, Mike and I had bedrooms that were next to each other. The walls between our bedrooms were really thin, and I could hear Mike staying up late at night with his radio turned on, playing with his tools and pretending he was an airplane pilot. There were lots of sound effects coming out from his bedroom.

"SHWOOOOOSHHHHHHHHHHHH...."

"This is your captain from the deck."

"NNNNEEEEEAAARRRROOOOMMMM ... we just flew over the ocean."

"BOOOMMMM...Vroommmm..."

"Mayday! Mayday! We just got hit! Mayday!"

"Tower control come in! Tower control come in!"

Mike could go on for hours roleplaying alone like this at night. It was fun to hear his imagination spring to life through the wall that divided us.

My family is not very expressive when it comes to how we feel about each other. We are a very traditional Chinese family and culturally, we were never taught to openly express our feelings for each other. I have never heard my mom or dad say "I love you" to each other, nor have they ever said it to us. Growing up, I always knew that love was something understood, expected, and practiced. I grew up seeing love as something that is within the actions of our being. Do I love my family? Of course, I do. Do I love my siblings? Of course, I do. But we did not say this to each other. Love is understood and expressed through actions, not words.

This unspoken love was definitely felt within my family. I remember hearing Mike talking to my mom many years after my accident, saying, "I would like to help her," pointing to me, "but she won't let me, and I don't know how to help. I'd like to help." His words struck my heart and made me think about my own actions and behaviors.

"Why didn't I let him?"

"Why did I not let anyone come close to me in those dark days and nights?"

"Why did I not allow people to help me?"

The answer I came up with was FEAR. Fear of losing control of the situation, fear of humiliation, fear of appearing incompetent or less intelligent, fear of seeming unsure or unprepared, and fear of being the one to stand out from the crowd with all eyes on me. All I wanted my entire life was to blend in, to be invisible and to not be seen with my physical challenges. It was the fear of being different and being unique.

Mike was not the only one I didn't allow to help me or get close to me. After the accident, I felt that in order for me to take control of my life, I needed to be strong. I couldn't let anyone down or cause them to feel disappointed about my inability to take care of myself. I didn't want to be seen as someone weak who needed the world to give her a helping hand in order to survive. I wanted to prove to everyone that I may look physically different, walk funny, and my legs may look disfigured, but I can do this alone. I can carry my own weight, I can lift my own luggage at the airport, I can open doors for myself. I don't need anybody. That's it: I DON'T NEED ANYBODY.

But the day Mike told my mom he had every intention of helping me, it created some self-awareness for me and I was able to reflect on all the judgments I carried about what it meant for me to be strong.

Mike never expressed any of his feelings about my accident until that day when he spoke with my mom. Listening to their conversation made me realize how selfish I had been to put a wall up between myself and my family, and in particular, with Mike. How selfish I was to think that I was the only person affected by this tragedy.

What happened to me didn't just happen to me,

but to everybody around me, too. I wish I had heard that conversation sooner after the accident, because it would have made me nicer—or at least more gentle, understanding, and compassionate toward my family. There is always something positive on the other side of the rainbow. The most valuable lesson I learned from my relationship with Mike was that when we let our guard down to allow those who are close to us step into our lives, we can do so much more than what we can do alone. There were times I needed a light bulb changed or to reach something high and heavy, and Mike never stopped helping me or lending an extra hand.

My sister Emily and I, on the other hand, had a different, much closer relationship than the one I had with Mike. Emily was only seven years old when my accident happened. She's the wild one in the family in the sense that she carefree-a true free spirit. She has a free spirit. One time when she was five, she was playing with a neighbor kid outside. It was five o'clock in the afternoon and Mom had just finished cooking dinner. Mike and I were already inside the house getting ready to eat, but Emily was nowhere to be found. Mom got mad and we all know that when Mom gets mad, we will *all* be in trouble. So, before my mom even said anything, Mike and I went out searching for Emily.

"Emily!" Mike and I yelled.

"Emily! Time for supper! Emily!"

We searched and searched, looking in all the places she could have possibly gone. Finally, after nearly 30 minutes of walking, we saw Emily running towards us, butt naked, happy, and smiling.

"Emily, where are your clothes?" Mike asked.

"Oh, they're by the pond." Emily replied.

"Why did you take them off? You can't just run around naked, you know!" Mike said.

"I got them wet when we were playing and I heard you calling me."

"Arrg... You're a girl! you can't do that! Shame on you!" Mike sounded frustrated.

The neighborhood where we grew up in Taiwan was safe. Crime rates were not so high back when we were kids, and many of us who were born before the '80s got to experience growing up in nature and spending a lot of time outdoors. Nonetheless, Mike was still very concerned about Emily's safety. Emily, on the other hand, didn't care at all. That night, Mom gave Emily a lecture on why it wasn't OK to be butt naked and running around in the neighborhood.

But that's just how Emily was; the kind of kid who went with the flow. During my recovery, Emily helped me with a lot of things that were out of my reach. In a sense, I took it for granted that she was always going to be there and give me the help that I needed.

Since she and I shared a bedroom, there were a lot of things we talked about at night before we went to sleep. We would watch TV together late into the night and talk about funny things that happened in school. Both my sister and I relished our inside jokes, including the naming of our next rescue dog, whom we called "Pee Pee," which means "fart" in Chinese.

Even though Emily and I spoke about many things, there were a few things she and I never discussed. Unlike other sisters, we never talked about boys or makeup. By the time she got into junior high school, I was already a high school student. It felt natural that, because I didn't have a normal body like other girls at the school, my physical appearance would not become a typical teenage preoccupation. Instead, I spent a lot of time focusing on my school work, my grades, and thinking about the university I wanted to go to. My world revolved around academics, and not the social aspect of high school life. As a result, I didn't know much about making myself look pretty by wearing better-fitting clothes or applying makeup. When my sister got to the age where she became conscious about her own body and looks, this conversation was missing between us. I couldn't offer her advice about boys or offer tips on how to apply makeup.

Fast forward into adulthood, when I was asked to represent our family and give a speech at Emily's wedding. I started off by telling everyone that I was not a very good sister to her. I never told her how pretty she was or how fortunate I was to have her in my life. I never taught her to apply makeup to make all the boys in her class want to date her. I never told her how much I worried about her when she had a 104-degree fever, and subsequently slipped and fell in the bathtub. And I admitted that I took it for granted that she would always be there when I needed her.

It's funny how we take so many things in life for granted. The people who show up in our lives—whether it's immediate family members or random strangers on the street— who lend us a helping hand. It's easy to take for granted that this is how the world is supposed to be. Locked in my own tragedy, I forgot that all those around me were just as connected to that life-altering event as I was. A butterfly flapping its wings in China does indeed create tornados in Russia. It wasn't until years later that I realized how selfish I had been, and what a horrible sister I was to my brother and my sister. They've loved me unconditionally all their lives, and loved me just the way I am. When the rest of my world is falling apart, I can always count on my family to be there for me. I am not alone.

Chapter

Eight

"Our triumph over sorrow is not that we can avoid it but that we can endure it. And therein lies our hope; that in spirit we might become bigger than the problems we face."

— Marianne Williamson,
Everyday Grace: Having Hope, Finding Forgiveness And Making Miracles

A fter I graduated from high school, I was accepted to the State University of New York at Stony Brook where I majored in Pharmacology and Chemistry. It was the first time living completely on my own. Living in a dorm wasn't quite as exciting as I hoped it would be; it turns out I had a lot of fear around living on campus by myself. I didn't know anybody, and I was so reliant on my family that it made me feel really insecure. The only time I was truly away from my family before this were the years I spent living in the rehab center. But things were different back then because people who lived in the rehab center were either just as unfortunate as I was, or, as was often the case, even worse than I was. Living in a dorm is different. What if I didn't like my roommate or we didn't get along?

Before the school semester began, we all received a list of items to bring from home, like bed sheets and comforters. The dorm was co-ed, so there would be guys possibly living very nearby. I had a lot of hopes and dreams about who I wanted to be at this time in my life. I wanted to start dating, to wear trendy clothes, and to enjoy taking long walks across campus without feeling pain in my back and bones. As I got older, I began noticing how bad posture could lead to permanent damage to my legs. I was still wearing those very ugly shoes, but life felt somewhat normal.

While many of my friends in college were already dating and going to parties every Thursday night, there was still a part of me thinking, "Of course, why would that guy like me when he has better choices?" and "I wish I could do that." I had some good male friends, but I never expressed affection toward them. I was afraid of being rejected and I was afraid of the looks in their eyes or the facial expressions that said they felt bad for me. I held my pride, and sure, I wanted to dress up every Thursday night and go across campus to hang out and truly enjoy a typical college life, but I couldn't. Not because I didn't want to, but because I didn't feel confident enough to walk into a place and be who I was. I didn't *know* who I was.

Instead, I spent four years at college focusing on things I knew I was good at: academics. I was the nerd in the class who took detailed notes at every lecture and went home to study them line by line. I was the one who spent nights in the library rather than doll myself up and be within the crowd. I knew I was smart, so I thought maybe there was someone out there who would be willing to look beyond my physical appearance and would like me the way I liked him.

It was during college that I discovered the beautiful world of the internet.

I met a lot of friends who were Computer Science majors who wrote programs and read codes, and they later influenced me to learn how to operate old IBM PC DOS computers and master Internet Relay Chat (IRC), which was the great grandfather of Messenger that so many of us use today.

Through the internet I was able to converse and express many of my feelings to people that I couldn't say in real life. There was a sense of comfort in the fact that they couldn't see me, and therefore they couldn't judge me for how I looked. I felt safer thinking that, for the first time, guys would actually get to know me for who I am on the inside instead of getting caught up in my physical differences. Meeting someone online was not a very common way to connect or develop romantic relationships back then, but it did the trick for me in the fact that I was not really looking for anyone to hook up with, but rather just someone to understand and listen to me, and someone who might potentially like me and be interested in learning more about me.

Although I was fascinated by how easy it was to connect with people around the world through the internet, I had bigger dreams. Because of my past experiences with hospitals, trauma, and years of rehabilitation, I was inclined to label myself a Pre-Med student. All my efforts throughout those four years of college were leading me to apply for medical school as the ultimate goal. I went to every lecture, took detailed notes, visited professors during office hours to build relationships for future recommendation letters, and I studied hard. By the time I finished college, my leg deformities had created enough pressure on my back that standing for too long or walking too far became painful. My legs were so weak sometimes that after I sat for a long time, I would have to get up and stand for a few moments before taking a first step.

My mom found out that I wanted to be a doctor and was supportive of the idea, but realistically she was very concerned about whether or not I was physically capable of meeting the requirements. She did what every mother making a choice out of fear would: she convinced me not to pursue a career as a doctor, suggesting instead that I work in a laboratory or choose another career where I would be able to sit. And she was so convincing in her efforts and the aches and pains in my body were so intense that I ultimately agreed that perhaps choosing Pre-Med wasn't really what I wanted. I second- guessed my ability to become anything greater.

In my third year of college, I shifted my goals. A stream of thoughts started to haunt me, like "maybe I don't want to be a doctor. What do I want to be if not a doctor?" or "What can I be if I am not a doctor?" I was already on the path of being a Science major with strong interests in chemistry and biochemistry. I completely flunked biology my freshman year, and thought it was meant to be because every Pre-Med student I met at the time was a Biology major. I barely passed that class with a C on my final exam. At the time, I wished English had been my first language, because I truly felt that had I been more fluent as a freshman, I probably would not have done as badly in biology. There were a lot of words in biology I didn't understand, and this kept me from taking better notes in class. You see, I have a tendency to do this. Whenever something bad happens to me, I immediately tell myself, "Of course this would happen to me." This was no different in an academic environment.

Coincidentally, in my junior year, an entirely new program called Pharmacology was developed. It was a good fit with the majority of the classes I was taking at the time, and switching majors at this point would not mean sacrificing the three years of study I'd already completed. After thinking it through, I dove right into a double major in Pharmacology and

Chemistry. One semester I worked for a German professor at a biochemistry lab on campus. My job was simple: culture some bacteria, put them in a petri dish, and let them grow. Afterward, I'd collect the bacteria and spin them down in a centrifuge machine and conduct some tests on them. This nine-to-five job where I got to sit most of the time was easy. I simply had to collect the data, analyze it, and report it to my professor. I needed this work to gain work experience as well as earn credits to expedite my graduation process.

That winter, I arranged a housing deal with a fellow student who would be away, leaving behind her empty dorm room, asking if I could sleep in her dorm room while working for the Biochemistry lab. She agreed, and it worked out pretty well—with one exception. One day, after a snowstorm, I woke up and proceeded to get ready for work, then walked myself down the stairs and into the parking lot. It was there that it happened: I slipped on a layer of ice right next to my car. It was very early in the morning during winter recess and there was no one around. I landed flat on my face, hitting my head on the ground. I managed to get up, find a non-slippery spot to steady myself on, at which point I felt a stream of warmth running down on my face. I wore glasses back then, so I took them off and saw they were broken. I raised my arm to wipe my face and knew I was bleeding excessively. I didn't panic, but slowly went back upstairs and dialed 911.

The dispatcher asked some routine questions and

luckily, the dormitory I was staying in at the time was close to the Health campus where we had our own university hospital. The ambulance arrived shortly afterward, and because I was still bleeding, the EMS brought the gurney to carry me out to the ambulance.

I surprised myself by not panicking when this accident happened. I was extremely calm, feeling as if there was another person inside me pulling me forward and lifting me up. A voice said, "Michelle, now you are going to get up and you are going to go upstairs to call for help." I followed the voice in the midst of everything that was happening—ne on the floor, glasses broken, bleeding excessively, and no one around to help. It was that voice that reminded me, "You are alone now. Get up and help yourself because no one else will." In that moment, I felt the strength that lived inside of me all along, but it was also in that moment that I felt very alone.

Chapter

Nine

"Hope is the thing with feathers, that perches in the soul and sings the tune without the words and never stops at all."

— Emily Dickinson, *The Complete Poems of Emily Dickinson*

After graduating from college with a double major in Pharmacology and Chemistry, I started to look for a job. My options were either spending all my energy looking for work in a laboratory, or going out and doing something different with my degrees. I wasn't sure what I could do with these degrees, so I started scouring newspaper ads searching for companies that wanted to hire people with chemistry backgrounds. One of the openings I came across was in Long Island, New York, close to where I lived. My parents had already helped me by buying a car for me when I was in college, so this job would be an easy commute. I applied and landed an interview with them.

You know how sometimes when you're about to do something new, and there's an enormous amount of fear that arrives at your doorstep, pounding on the door and demanding to come in to talk you out of whatever you're doing? So, the day of my interview at this company, my fear showed up and wanted to talk me out of this. I did what others might also do when they are afraid: I brought someone close to me to the interview, hoping that their presence would make me feel safer and give me more confidence. That day, my mom drove with me to the interview. I know—it's a paradox. One day I have the strength to walk up two flights of stairs, bloody face and all, to call an ambulance for myself, and the next minute I need my mom for emotional support. But the truth is that after my accident, I felt safest around my family. I knew they would never judge me for how I look, and that I could always count on them to be there for me. I could depend on them when I felt alone.

I was experiencing fear as a fresh college graduate out in the world alone for the first time. It was the fear of the unknown world I was stepping into—a new chapter in my life that was about to begin. Besides feeling a bit frightened, there was also a sense of excitement; I was looking forward to new life experiences.

My appearance and the fact that I looked different became a label I put onto myself. I didn't like my picture taken. In fact, I couldn't even look at my own photograph. Short, wobbly penguin walk, crooked legs; my body looked funny. But yet, like everyone else, I wanted to be loved. I wanted to be seen and heard. I wanted to have a normal life where I could blend in. But no matter where I went or who I was with, I always stood out. I was afraid of the way people looked at me—afraid of seeing them feeling sorry for me, and fearful that my physical condition would prevent me from fulfilling my role on the job. The concerns that a future employer might have about hiring me were showing up in my own fears.

Fear plays an important role in our lives; it compels us to slow down and think before we act. Fear can also be a detriment, thought, keeping us from trying new things or reaching out full potential. I was afraid of being judged for the way I looked, and so many of the decisions I have made in life were based upon the fear of being viewed as incapable. In many ways, fear ruled my life.

The company I interviewed with produced Boeing 747 engines. They were looking for someone with a chemistry background to fill a management position. The staff appeared overwhelmingly male, tall, and muscular. As I waited to be called in for the interview, self-judgement showed up.

"What was I thinking, applying for this position? I can't do this job. They wouldn't want to hire me." My internal dialog was doing a great job in making me second guess myself. I did not get the job. Looking back to the memory now, had I shown up feeling differently about myself and believed in my qualifications and abilities, I have no doubt they would have hired me on the spot. If I was incapable of feeling good about myself, how could I expect others to have faith in me?

For many years, I hid away as much as possible so I wouldn't be noticed. I lived in a world full of embarrassments, struggles, doubts, and low self-esteem. I was afraid to speak up because I thought my English-language skills weren't good. I was afraid to repeat myself when people asked me to say a sentence one more time. I was afraid to try on fitted pants because I was sure they would never look good on me.

Confidence can only come from within. It requires us to have a clear sense of who we are and who we want to be. It requires us to go through that internal transformation from being invisible to being invincible. Confidence is knowing what you're good at, the value you provide, and behaving in ways that conveys that to others. It is different from arrogance or believing you are better than you are in a particular area. Confidence is also different from low self-esteem, which involves believing you are less valuable than you think you are.

Confidence is not shallow. It's a deep sense of self-awareness that makes you feel OK even without clothes or other modern-day armor we use to cover ourselves. Everyone feels a lack of self-confidence from time to time, but we need to get to a place where we are truly, authentically ourselves without the masks, and be comfortable in own skin.

I was nowhere close to feeling confident. And with the lack of confidence, I began using negative self-talk—words that, if were to say them to another person, I would probably be sent to jail. Things like, "Why are you still alive?"and "You are not wanted" and "Look at you. What makes you think this guy would want to be with you?" There were many nights after falling asleep that I'd wake up crying and wishing I was never born.

Chapter

Ten

"Life's under no obligation to give us what we expect."

— Margaret Mitchell, *Gone with the Wind*

After applying for multiple jobs failing multiple interview processes, I began considering that perhaps I needed a new set of skills to live a life of financial independence from my parents. With my degrees, the only option that would save me time and spare me having to repeat coursework I had already completed was applying to Pharmacy school. Pharmacy was not very popular at the time, but one of my high school classmates had gone to Pharmacy school after graduation. I knew I was good at studying, and Pharmacy was the closest I could get to becoming a doctor. Perhaps pursuing a career in Pharmacy would be a good alternative to sustain myself.

The following academic year, I was accepted into pharmacy school at St John's University.

This was in 1993—a time when the internet was becoming a popular new tool, and there was a shift in the use of technology, whereby we moved from an antiquated IBM DOS system to a more sophisticated Windows 95 system. I had returned home to live with my parents after undergraduate schooling and during those early days of dial-up, I could spend hours on the internet holding the phone line hostage. While I did manage to make some friends during Pharmacy school—and am still in touch with many of them today—what really opened the door to allow me to see other parts of the world were my interactions on the internet.

I spent most of my free time in chat rooms connecting with people from my home country. We talked and laughed at each other's jokes, and I took comfort in the fact that we were all complete strangers to each other. With this quasi-anonymity, I was able to share many of the inner thoughts that I tended to hold back from sharing with friends and even my own family. I was afraid of what people would say if they discovered there was a part of me that didn't match their perceptions of me. My circle of friends and even my own family in real life often see me as a confident and optimistic person, with a bright and caring personality. But even the happiest person in the world will experience sadness, loneliness, and negative thoughts. No one is immune from the feelings of anxiety, nervousness, fear, or struggle. But I hid my emotions so well that many of my close friends didn't know the other side of me, hiding in the dark, withdrawn, alone, and sad.

It was as if I was perpetually wearing two masks; the one I wanted people to see and the one I shared with strangers who couldn't see me and judge me. Whenever my friends asked me if I was feeling OK, I would reply with a quick, "Yeah, I'm OK" or "I'm fine." I rarely spoke the truth about how I felt, and I was under the impression that no one truly cared, anyway.

The virtual world was a safe ground for me to express my inner thoughts and feelings—the dark secrets I wouldn't share with family and friends out of fear of disappointing them. I was hiding from the reality of who I was.

I started blogging early on in Pharmacy school after learning to write the complicated html code needed to create a standard and functional webpage. I interacted and made friends from Taiwan, many of whom I'm still in contact with today. I also fell in love with someone on the internet that I didn't know would eventually break my heart.

I was 24 years old and It was my first semester of Pharmacy school when everything was still very slow, and classes weren't challenging. I met Sean through an online Taiwanese chat group, and we exchanged messages and spent more and more time chatting and sharing thoughts on a daily basis. Sean was eight years older than me, and he owned a computer store in Taipei that built and repaired computers and offered troubleshooting services. I told him about my accident and all the challenges I faced in the years since. Sean was compassionate, and I had the sense he understood me and accepted me for who I was. Six months later, we decided to meet.

I lied to my parents, telling them that I was going to visit relatives in Taiwan after nearly 10 years living in the States. I also told my parents that I was going to be staying with a "friend" for the first few days so I could visit Taipei a little bit. I was so good at hiding my darkness—the part of me that I didn't want to share with my family and friends—that it was easy for me to make up a story about why I wanted to go back to Taiwan. In my mind, I was secretly working out all the logistics in case I ended up marrying this guy. It felt important, and I thought he could really be the person for me—the one who accepted me fully and didn't mind that I wasn't the perfect height or that my body wasn't the perfect shape. I thought he was the perfect one for me. I flew back during that summer after my first semester in Pharmacy school and stayed at his place. We talked, we laughed, and I lost my virginity to him during the first few days of my stay in Taiwan.

After a week, Sean and I parted ways but remained in close contact through telephone and the internet. By the time I returned to the United States and moved back in with my parents, I noticed things began to change a bit between us. He was not as warm as he used to be, and he invited his female friends to stay overnight on occasion and I didn't trust him when he told me they were just friends. My jealousy took over within the first month or two and I felt hopeless because I was not physically there to spy on him. I was angry, needy, and emotional.

There were days where I would call him multiple times and, when I'd reach his answering machine, I'd just become angrier and more resentful. I felt ashamed—ashamed for lying to my parents, and for giving the most important part of myself to someone who seemed to be as bad as everyone else I met, if not worse. I spent hours in the shower crying and scrubbing myself so hard in an attempt to wash away the shame that I carried.

One night after coming home from school, I was standing in the bathtub, water coming out of the showerhead dripping down my body. I scrubbed myself with an exfoliating sponge again and again and again, until my skin was tinted red. I came across a razor on top of the bathtub, picked it up. I thought about all the things that had happened to me, from the day of the accident, the pain I endured on those dreadful nights, and the hopelessness I felt deepening inside of me as a result of world's cruelty and the injustices done to me. My tears dropped like a rainfall, but I sobbed quietly, hiding behind the sound of running water over my head. With the knowledge of human anatomy I acquired in school, I knew exactly how to use this razor if I wanted to end things. I held the razor in one hand and thoughts of all the people in my life—Mom, Dad, Emily, Mike, my friends from school—flashed through my mind.

"How could I disappoint them like this? Are you sure about this?" I asked myself.

With that thought, I got scared. I was scared of my own suicidal ideas.

I was afraid to disappoint my family and friends. The same fear that had showed up for me when I walked into a public area and people turned to look at me was the same fear I am having now holding the razor in front of me.

"I don't want to die." I told myself.

I felt like I needed to tell someone about this. I needed to tell someone how I felt and about all the darkness I held inside throughout my life. What would they think of me? Probably something along the lines of, "Oh, Michelle just get over it." Or perhaps they'd be mad at me—especially my parents. I dropped the razor, which made a clicking sound as it hit the surface of the tub.

The following few mornings, I'd wake up feeling a heaviness in my chest, carrying it around while appearing to be doing business as usual. By nightfall, I'd find myself having dreams about falling and would wake up in panic, then cry myself to sleep quietly to avoid waking my sister and the rest of my family members.

I needed help but I didn't know who I could go to and ask for help, so I went on, business as usual, with my life.

I went into work the following day after my classes,

accepting prescriptions at the pharmacy windows, greeting customers, answering the telephone and questions from the public, filling subscriptions, and pulling drugs from the shelves. No one needed to know what had happened to me the night before.

After returning from my trip to Taiwan, I had found a pharmacy internship position at a large pharmacy chain. The way I got that job was a coincidence and I considered myself lucky to have landed it. I discovered they were hiring at a local drugstore through a friend who had just been hired there. The pharmacy manager wasn't there the day of my interview, so instead, the store manager, Jose, interviewed me. He was about 5 feet 8 with curly short hair, coffee-colored skin, chocolate brown eyes and he was very friendly. Jose must have really liked what I said during the interview because he hired me on the spot.

The next day I got a call from Katie, the pharmacy manager, who told me that there'd been a mistake and that they did not need me in the store. For a moment I was really disappointed, but then she said that, since it was a mistake on their part, she could transfer me to a similar position at another store if I was willing to travel. I took the offer and she sent me off to Long Island City, Queens, just 10 minutes away from Manhattan.

Three months after contemplating suicide, the heaviness was still pressing down on my chest; feelings of being hurt and the hatred towards myself. I began crying halfway through my shift. I didn't tell anyone—*couldn't* tell anyone. Being vulnerable takes courage. In fact, it takes more than just courage; it takes love for oneself and the kind of compassion we so willingly offer other people, and the strength to know that it is OK to share your story with others. We can survive being judged by the looks in their eyes, the expressions on their faces, and the distances they keep. Vulnerability is not a weakness, but a strength that allows us to tell our story as it is. I wasn't yet ready to share that with the world. Not in that moment.

Instead, I turned my vulnerability into poetry and blog posts. Those tearful nights turned into words of solace. I started journaling and filling pages of my diary with my thoughts. I kept them in my closet where I could spend hours flipping through the pages to reread them over days, months, and years. The more I wrote about my thoughts, the more I became aware of this duality: There were my thoughts, and then there was me. I became curious about exploring the deeper meaning of "self."

Chapter

Eleven

"Are you proud of yourself tonight
that you have insulted a total
stranger whose circumstances you
know nothing about?"

— Harper Lee, *To Kill a Mockingbird*

I made some really good friends during my Pharmacy school years. Mostly Asian Americans born and raised in the United States, and the more I hung out with them, the more fluent my English became. We all took a summer off in 2000 and flew ourselves to Jamaica, spending a week together before we graduated. It was the first time in my life traveling to a foreign country without my family. It was here in Jamaica that, for the first time, I discovered I was a happy drunk.

The last two years of Pharmacy school was the time I really came alive. I was getting more comfortable speaking to people, and the group of friends I was hanging out with really saw me for who I was. We'd skip out from our classes sometimes to hang out at local restaurants. I always parked close to our classroom buildings because of my handicap privilege parking space. Five or six of us would jump into my car, and I ended up being the designated driver. My friends made fun of my driving skills all the time, but we always had a great time and lots of laughs together.

Most of my friends were in relationships already, and over time, I got to know their significant others. One friend, Kim, mentioned the idea of setting me up with a guy she knew. I was skeptical, but agreed I'd give it a try. Kim proposed introducing us at a party at her house the following weekend. I was nervous but also kind of excited about what was to come.

Sometimes we form judgments about ourselves as well as others, and these judgments create barriers that prevent us from connecting with people. On the day of Kim's party, I went over to her house and noticed some guy who was physically challenged who had joined our group. And just like that, from the moment he walked into the room to the moment I left the house, I didn't look at him nor speak a word to him.

What was going on within myself was the very same reaction other people often experience when *I* walk into a room.

"*She* looks different."

"I wonder what's wrong with her?"

"Oh, that poor thing."

"She's handicapped. How sad."

Those very same judgments people direct toward me where the ones I was pressing on him. I also felt insulted that my friends would set me up with someone who wasn't "normal." It hurt and disappointed me, because what I was saying to myself was, "Well, of course. I'm broken, and therefore you would set me up with someone who is also broken."

I was upset and felt insulted by Kim's good intentions. And all that judgment against that guy led to me completely ignoring his existence. I'm pretty sure it felt awkward for him too, but I didn't want to equate myself someone who wasn't "normal." Being with someone who is also physically challenged was the *last* thing I wanted. My pride, my anger, and my self-esteem stopped me from getting to know that person *as a person*, kept me from learning about his challenges, about what inspires him, and what makes him unique.

I was afraid that being seen with someone who was also physically challenged would make me feel further away from being "normal." No matter where we'd go, who we'd meet, or what happened in life, people would always have that judgment against us. I didn't like to be judged by people who based their understanding of me on my appearance, but yet here I was, judging him for how he looked rather than for who he was.

Years later, as I looked back at that set up that Kim had attempted during my Pharmacy school years, I felt ashamed by the things I said and did to another perfectly beautiful human being. Could I have been a little more kind to someone who had clearly gone through challenges with his physical limitations as I had? Could I have been a little more compassionate to another human being? Could I have been a little more open to accepting that person as my friend? Could I be less judgmental about myself and others?

The greatest triumph in becoming who I am is learning from my own mistakes and forgiving myself for having made them, and drawing value from the past to help me move forward.

Chapter

Twelve

"Courage is the most important of all the virtues because without courage, you can't practice any other virtue consistently."

— Maya Angelou, *Senior Convocation,*
May 24, 2008, Schoellkopf Stadium,
Cornell University

While living at home during pharmacy school, I learned to connect with my own family. My sister had been accepted to NYU in 1996 and also lived at home while commuting to school every day. My brother got into Radiology school in Brooklyn and he, too, was commuting to campus every day.

My dad has always been a big proponent of family

dinners together, and whenever we were all home, we'd make sure dinner was served at the dining table, and we wouldn't begin eating until everyone in the family was present. We wouldn't necessarily talk to each other during the meal, since our family isn't the type to share personal anecdotes about our day or ask about feelings, but we did it because it was important to Dad that we all be together at mealtimes.

In 2000, during my third year in Pharmacy school, my sister got into Boston University to study law. Emily took out a loan and rented a small apartment in downtown Boston. I drove her to her new home, along with our parents, and after I dropped her off at her new place that day, I cried on our way home and felt kind of silly because usually it's the mother dropping off her child at school who does the crying. I cried because, for the longest time, Emily was my little sister, the one I got to boss around when we were young, the one who sat in front of my little blackboard and pretended to be my student on no-school days, and the one who I sometimes fought with, pulling her hair and tearing her t-shirt. Watching her leave home and start her own life was bittersweet.

We all have strings attached; strings that connect us to our families, our friends, and all of those around us in everyday life. The bonds we form through our daily interactions determine how strong those strings are and how far they can be stretched. My sister was born on a winter's day, early in the morning, and when my dad walked into our room to wake us up to drive to the midwife's home, that was the day my sister and I became attached. Our lives interconnected with each other. She was there helping me through those difficult times when I could only reach so far into my plaster cast. She was there in the car driving with my parents every weekend to visit me in the rehabilitation center. But above all, Emily was the youngest child in our family, and I felt like a parent suddenly experiencing empty nest syndrome—that feeling of grief and loneliness parents feel when their youngest child leaves home for the first time to be on their own. Emily is that child to me.

The sisterhood string got stretched on that day when she first moved out of the house to live on her own. I wondering to myself what life would be like without her sleeping in the same room with me at night. The feeling of being lost and not knowing what the future holds wasn't something foreign to me. I felt the same way the first night my parents checked me into the rehabilitation center.

I worked every weekend throughout Pharmacy school. I attended classes Monday through Friday, and sometimes, after school, I would go into the store and work for a couple of hours. We needed to obtain work experience before we could take the board exam. I worked hard to accumulate those hours and made sure I had them in my book ready to go before applying to take the board exam.

There was an old pharmacist, Denny, whom I would often work with at the pharmacy. Big, tall, and Greek, he was in his 60s and almost ready to retire, partly because of his health issues. He used to own his own pharmacy in the early '80s, but ended up selling it to a big chain store—the same one we both worked for when I met him. Most of the time when we worked the same shift, I ended up doing all the work: taking in prescription orders, filling the orders, ringing the customer up at the register, and troubleshooting any technical problems we encountered during the shift. Denny was really nice, but I'd seen him roaming the aisle with the incontinence pads, and he smelled sometimes. I pretended not to notice because I knew he was embarrassed about it.

Denny taught me a lot when I was in Pharmacy school. He knew a lot of home remedies that worked like magic; if someone was experiencing diarrhea and didn't want to take the prescription medication, he offered an alternative remedy. He knew what might be good for a stomach ache or a teething baby, too. Because of his size, there were times he couldn't bend or reach areas between the shelves, and I was his go-to person. He saw the value in our work relationship during our shifts together. I felt important and needed when I worked with him. Denny taught me many things, not just in the pharmacy world, but also in real life.

He taught me how to take things lightly and not make them personal. He was a good example of not letting ego get in the way, having made the transition from business owner to employee at his own company and being managed by someone half his age. This wouldn't be an easy transition for anyone but Denny made it through OK. He still had his pride, and I only saw him get upset with a customer once, saying he wished it was his own store so he could have thrown that person out. I've also learned how to be compassionate towards others and to listen to what people have to say before making suggestions or recommendations.

While losing the connection and strong bond with my sister when she moved away, I refocused my attention on school, work, and getting my internship hours. I also channeled my energy into building relationships with other human beings. I am a firm believer of the old saying that when the universe closes one door, another door opens. In that constant flow within the universe, the moment we lose something or someone, something else steps into our lives and replaces what was lost. It could be another person or object of our affection or it could be an idea that arises in our subconscious mind, and from it, out grows a new possibility. We have the option to choose how we want to see the changes in our lives. We can see it as a loss, grief over what is lost, or the pain that comes from loss, and yet still embrace it with our open arms to welcome the new possibilities that rise up on the horizon.

Chapter

Thirteen

"Instructions for living a life.
Pay attention. Be astonished. Tell
about it."

— Mary Oliver, *Red Bird*

I worked at the retail pharmacy store throughout my entire undergraduate Pharmacy program and into the first year of my graduate program. After receiving my bachelor's degree in Pharmacy, I took the board exam and became a licensed pharmacist working full time. Unfortunately, the supply of pharmacists in the area was becoming saturated, and I was unable to get assigned to a permanent store close to home. I became what they call a "floater"—a licensed pharmacist who works at stores where we are needed. Almost every day I would travel to a different store within the New York metropolitan area.

Many retail chains such as CVS, Walgreens, or Target have pharmacy departments located inside the store, often at the very back. By law, pharmacies need to be located where all medications are stored in a high-security area. To meet the requirement, retail chain stores design pharmacies with double-lock systems. One evening, just past 10 o'clock, I was closing at one of the stores in the Bronx. We'd had a very busy day. The store was right near a subway station, making it very convenient for customers to walk in and drop off a prescription that needed filling. As my intern and I were pulling down the roller gate above the cash register counter which served as our double-locked gate, I heard footsteps running past the pharmacy. My intern and I didn't think much of it and proceeded to count the day's cash receipts. I gathered all the money in the register and opened the door, preparing to hand over the cash and daily report to the store manager. Just then, I realized something was terribly wrong. A rifle was pointing directly at my head and a commanding voice yelled "Freeze!" I suppose my height was an advantage this day, since it made me appear harmless. I was at a standstill until the NYPD asked me if anyone else was inside the pharmacy with me. "Just my intern," I replied. We were both escorted outside the store.

As the remaining store employees were escorted outside, we were told to remain standing outside in front of the store. Finally, a police officer came to speak with us, saying two men had come into the store and held a number of night staff hostage. They broke open the safe and ran away with a couple thousand dollars. There were still people locked in the back room while NYPD searched the perimeter of the store looking for the perpetrators.

It was now nearing midnight on a cold winter's night in New York City, with rain and sleet coming down, and my intern and I were anxiously waiting to get back inside and pack up our stuff to go home. Finally, one by one, people were dismissed and allowed to leave. As I drove home, it finally occurred to me that, had I closed the gate even 10 minutes later than I did, I would have been among those people locked up in the back room.

A week after the incident, the district manager reached out to me and asked me if I was OK to go back to the store to cover some shifts. I was terrified. It wasn't until the day after the incident that I comprehended how serious an event it was, and felt the shock of having an NYPD rifle pointed at my head. I never liked going to that store anyway, so in a way I was glad that it happened on a night that I was there. If anything positive came out of it, it was that I could use the incident as a ticket to get me out of ever returning.

I am short, but I work efficiently. And I think because I was able to work efficiently, many of the pharmacy managers liked having me around. I spent a lot of time on the road after getting my pharmacist's license. The district manager I was working with at the time noticed my strength and ability to handle high-volume stores, so he floated me to many busy stores that were farther away from home; 25 miles north in Yonkers, or even as far as New City, more than an hour's drive away in the northern part of the Tri-State Area. At first, I didn't mind the drive at all; it was actually quite nice to drive to New City across the George Washington Bridge, crossing over into New Jersey. In the fall, the Palisades Parkway was lined with maple trees that turn vivid shades of orange and red, and in summer, beautiful greenery lined the parkway. In the winter, chandelier-like ice covers the tree branches. There was a sense of calm and peace every time I drove through this area.

During my last year of graduate school, one of my classmates took a position as a manager at a hospital in uptown Manhattan. We were chatting one day after class and I mentioned my interest in transitioning into a hospital setting. They happened to have a position opening and it was a perfect opportunity for me to try something new, so I took a leap of faith and jumped on it. I was scared. This was something very different from what I had done during my entire Pharmacy school curriculum, but it was definitely something I had wanted to do since college. This was really the closest I could get to my original plan of becoming a doctor. Well, technically I would still be a doctor by the time I finished my graduate program, but just not a medical doctor. To be able to work in a hospital setting had been my dream, so when the opportunity presented itself, it only made sense to accept my friend's offer.

What was really inconvenient about the position was the location. The idea of driving and parking in uptown Manhattan was absolutely horrifying to me. I was going to school full time, and after school, I would drive to the city and work for eight hours, not getting home until almost midnight every day. Everything in the pharmacy was "adult sized," meaning things were stored up high, and even the work bench was a little too tall for me. I ended up asking for a step stool to stand on so I'd be level with the workstation. But somehow I managed, despite all the challenges.

These challenges taught me that in order to get what I wanted, I needed to be very creative about how to go about achieving it. To reach things that were too high, I grabbed a chair and stood on it. When I was laughed at or discriminated against, I just needed to stand strong and defend myself. I learned that in order for people to see me for who I was, I needed to excel in whatever it was I was doing, and then some. I need to not only be good at something, but I needed to be the best.

Chapter

Fourteen

"It was better to know the worst than
to wonder."

— Margaret Mitchell, *Gone with the Wind*

I learned a lot about myself over the course of five years in Pharmacy school. As I started blogging, I discovered the part of me that was never revealed to the world. Every night when I got home, I would turn on my computer and log into my website, then begin by writing about the feelings I was having, things that happened during the day, the major events that transpired, and my emotions around them. It was an online diary that I shared with other friends I met online. I listened to music. I *love* music. There were many nights when I would tune into a radio station, plug in my earphones, and listen to music while my fingers flowed across the keyboard.

My parents made sure they exposed us to art early in life and this included music, which I grew up listening to in our house. After my accident, I was home more often than my siblings, and I was the one who had more patience to sit in front of a piano than my brother and sister. Therefore, my parents decided to send me to piano lessons. My piano teacher was tough. She held pencils in her hand and made sure that my fingers were always on the keys, in perfect position and form; fingers couldn't be flat on the keyboard; they needed to be formed as if I was holding onto a ball, slightly bent, and my fingernails had to be trimmed short. Any deviations from the proper form and she would hit my knuckles with the pencil. If you have ever hit your funny bone, you know how painful that feels. There's nothing funny about hitting those funny bones or having your fingers hit with a pencil.

When I left Taiwan for the United States, my parents couldn't afford to get me a piano, so for a long time, I didn't play, but music never left my life. I liked singing and think this profound appreciation of music came from my mom. When we were little, I used to hear her singing all the time. She would hum something when she walked around with my sister in her arms, lulling her to sleep. When she cooked, she would hum songs as she prepared our meals.

After Emily graduated from law school, my parents decided that they would like to move to the

West Coast and be close to my grandparents who were in their late 70s at the time. My sister was able to find a job working for my aunt's law office and I was in the process of taking the California Pharmacy Board license exam.

"You're not a good test taker."

That was the message I told myself at the time. And this message was so powerful that indeed, when I took the exam on the first try, I failed miserably. Our house in New York was sold; my uncle bought us out, and we used the money from the sale to pay for our move to California. My family rented a house from my aunt Shelly at first. The rent was cheap, and the house was in decent shape. There were two bedrooms, even though we really needed three, so I ended up using a curtain to create a makeshift bedroom in one section of the dining room. What right did I have to ask for a bedroom? Had I passed the Board exam, I would have probably found a job already and had some savings. But, no. I failed the test and couldn't retake it until the following year.

On those dark nights I found myself sinking into the deepest emotional turmoil, wallowing in the pain and suffering I bore since the accident, from the failure of my relationship with Sean in Taiwan, and now, the anxiety that came with the fact that I didn't pass the Board exam. All the things that could go wrong, *did* go wrong in my life.

I would spend hours in front of the keyboard translating those invisible feelings into words. I also found an online radio station in Taiwan that I logged into and interacted with new friends overseas, connecting with them through the exchange of words. It was that feeling of "I am not alone" that brought me comfort. Before I realized it, I made a number of friends through my blog and the chat room I visited online that was connected to the radio station. It was almost as if I was living two different lives; one outside of the internet where friends saw me as this fun and happy person, and one on the internet where friends saw me as this sentimental being with talent and artistic skills in poetry and writing.

It was during those times spent on the blog and in the radio station chatroom that I met my best friend for life, Johnny. He was a very talented music composer by day and worked as a radio DJ at night for a station in Taiwan. I was one of his many fans following him on the chatroom. We talked online and offline, and during our chats, I learned that he grew up in the States and later moved back to Taiwan after graduating from college. We had quite a number of things in common, including music. Our friendship developed into something more, and eventually, I started writing lyrics for him and Johnny would do his magic in translating those words into music.

I wrote letters to Johnny; more specifically, they were love letters. Initially I wrote them on the blog and categorized them as "love letters." Each letter followed a specific music theme, a song we had talked about, or an inspiration around music. Those letters then became handwritten journal entries; every word I blogged about on the internet was transcribed into a notebook, and every time I filled a notebook, I would mail it across the sea to him. They weren't just love letters, but also words of encouragement, thoughts, feelings, and emotions. They were our everyday lives and challenges that we both had to face, and the valuable lessons that we could each learn from them. Every single incident and feeling of connection was real. It was strange to have such a strong connection with someone whom I had never met in person, but yet I had the sense that he understood me, and he heard me.

You know that feeling when you get to know someone but feel you really don't know them that well? I felt that about him sometimes. It sometimes seemed like he was not sharing everything with me, and finally after years of keeping those feelings to myself, I gathered my courage and confronted him. We talked and he finally told me that he could not reciprocate his feelings for me because of his sexual preference. Yup! He finally came out of the closet and told me how he tried to make it work, but just couldn't.

I was shocked. I felt angry and I felt betrayed. With all our years of friendship, he couldn't have the decency to tell me that he's gay? And there I was, thinking all along that it was *my* problem.

In the beginning I was angry. I was angry that he didn't tell me sooner and that he took me and the true feelings and love I had for him for granted. Would I have been less angry with him had he told me earlier? Probably. But it also got me to think about that friendship we had. It was pure and genuine; it was sincere and true. I learned to see it from his perspective; the shame and burden he had to carry with him when he wasn't yet out of the closet. Stepping out of our comfort zones is not something any one of us could just easily do. It requires courage, strength, and bravery to finally let things go.

A year and a half later after I passed the Board exam and found a job at a university hospital, I went back to Taiwan for a visit. Even though I grew up in Taiwan, I knew very little about it. There were places I didn't go because of the lingering childhood memories of being in the rehabilitation center. I never had an elementary graduation ceremony; I didn't know what it was like to spend a Saturday afternoon hanging out with friends from school, eating ice cream and watching a movie together. And I didn't know what it was like to like somebody in junior high school, getting dressed up and going out on a movie date. I wanted to experience all that. All the things that I missed, all the memories I didn't have—I wanted to experience them and revisit all the places I knew growing up.

A few days before I got on the plane, I reached out to Johnny. I wrote him an email and told him that I was going to Taiwan for a visit. If he was interested, I would like to meet up while I was in town. I had been angry when we stopped communicating with each other. The anger that lit up inside of me was so strong that I was not expecting that he would respond at all, but he did. You know how some friends you never really call or see very often, but when you do meet, you pick up right where you left off? He gets you and you get him; you don't need to explain too much to each other—things are just kind of understood between you. That is the kind of friendship I had—and still have—with Johnny; pure, true, and loyal. Did I love him? Yes. I still love him like a friend, a brother, a sister, a friend whom I know will someday show up at my funeral crying. This is the kind of friendship I have with Johnny. Recently, he tagged me on a Facebook post and we had a short online conversation. I asked him how long we had known each other.

"18 years," he typed.

I went into silence and didn't respond with any more words.

Chapter

Fifteen

"Lock up your libraries if you like;
but there is no gate, no lock, no bolt
that you can set upon the freedom of
my mind."

— Virginia Woolf, *A Room of One's Own*

As I continued writing my blog and using it as a dumping ground for my emotions, the more I noticed the changes happening within me. I became more self-aware, and there was an urge to read more about this inner world of mine that I had never truly explored. I was able to connect with a number of like-minded people online who were also bloggers who devoted themselves to writing, and we all shared some common beliefs: life is all suffering and everything is a challenge.

I worked the night shift at the hospital, and in the mornings, I would spend a few hours managing my blog. The schedule worked out well for some time, but eventually, I started to feel burned out at work. It was a tertiary transplant hospital, meaning many of the things we'd do involved critically ill patients. Lots of phone calls throughout the day and lots of frustration from colleagues and other healthcare professionals.

I was hired by a director, Steve—a man in his late forties—along with the manager of the pharmacy, April, who was in her sixties. Steve was a successful, determined, and goal-oriented businessperson who could be intimidating at times, and when he first hired me, I was afraid of him. Despite my impressions of Steve, he had a good heart and cared about his employees. A colleague of mine recently told me that the day Steve hired me, he ran out of his office to announce it to everyone and he went to see the pharmacy buyer, Karen, to ask her about placing an order.

"I just hired a short person. Let's order some step stools," he said.

Two other girls were hired around the same time I was, and both of them had been working in this department as interns before. As you can probably imagine, it fired up a lot of insecurities I had about myself. I didn't graduate from the same school they did, I hadn't worked there as an intern, and wasn't familiar with the staff already working there. I definitely didn't have the look that they did, and sometimes I felt isolated because they had their own clique. And because of these insecurities, I told myself I had to watch everything I did and think about who I needed to acquaint myself with in order to keep my job and make myself visible in the workplace.

Working at this hospital was not an easy job. The environment was fast-paced, and at night there was significant work that needed to be done. Many of the staff had strong personalities, and I sometimes felt they were not really open to people coming in from outside of their circle. They tended to be extra harsh on anyone who intruded. One day I was working my shift as usual and must have processed a doctor's order off the protocol, and one of my colleagues called me on the phone and spoke to me in a condescending tone. I felt hurt, attacked, and shamed into feeling small about myself. In that moment, I dropped all my tasks at hand and got out of the pharmacy as fast I could, locking myself in the bathroom where I broke down in tears.

Suddenly, it hit me was that no matter how hurt I felt or how long I allowed myself to cry in the bathroom, none of this mattered to the person verbally attacking me. I could spend hours crying and feeling sorry for myself, or I could dry my tears and go out there and continue to work; I could fight through this or give up. The reality hit me like a thunderbolt; where am I going to find another job? It took me so long to pass the Board exam and finally land a job here. What would I do? Should I continue to work in an environment where I was treated like an outsider, didn't feel supported, and where no one seemed to respect me?

I chose to stay.

I played along to get along.

I started getting to know people who worked the night shift. I'd sit with them during our break time, go out from time to time to have late night snack after work, share conversations about our lives outside the hospital, and we'd bring each other small gifts. I'd sometimes pump them for information about my colleagues to get more insights about their personalities. What are they like when they're working the morning shift? Who do I need to watch out for or stay away from in order to protect myself and stay out of trouble?

I felt lucky because the night-shift crew tended to be less intimidating and were easier to work with than the daytime staff, as long as I did my part. As soon as a day shift opened up, I asked to be moved. The day-shift crew had completely different personalities and more drama that I needed to deal with. During this time, I learned and I was a fast learner. I learned to get along with people and stay as low-key as possible, but sometimes I still got myself into trouble.

Life had become a routine at this point. Going to work and coming home from work. There were a few dramatic episodes at home and at work, but nothing exciting to talk about to anyone. When I first got out of pharmacy school, I felt empowered—like there was a purpose in my life and that I was going to make a living out of this and be someone important.

Throughout the years, that vision of being someone important started to fade away. Working for a large corporation did not help alleviate this feeling inside of me. In fact, it became more obvious to me when an administrative management position opened up, and I began thinking I had a chance at getting the job. Later I found out a good friend of mine, Cindy, also decided to apply for the same position.

With the news that Cindy was applying for the same position, I began to experience one of those moments of uncertainty again. Right when I was on the precipice of a move up in a new and interesting direction, doubt started creeping in. There are voices in our heads that follow us like shadows that we can't hide from. On a good day, if we are lucky, the voices tell us something positive and nice; but other days, they can be quite noisy, saying things that just make you feel exhausted.

"Watch, she's going to get that position, not you."

"I wonder if she's doing this because she likes competition."

"Why is she even doing this? I thought she wasn't even interested. Bitch!"

When you hear these voices often enough, you start to think they might be speaking truth.

The idea of having an inner critic—a monster that lives inside of our heads—is not a new concept to anyone. We all have one and we all listen to it from time to time. Over the last few years, many well-known authors and thinkers have discussed it; Oprah talks about it; Eckhart Tolle teaches people about it; and Buddhism, Christianity, and other religions discuss the idea of the inner critic and how human consciousness is affected by it.

However, what many people fail to recognize is that it is not just the "voice in your head," the "inner critic," or the "gremlin" that you have to pay attention to; the ultimate goal is to recognize its purpose and the power it has over you when it shows up. How do you tame the voice in your head while keeping it in the passenger seat?

Prior to my interview for the management position, Cindy and I talked. She and I became close friends throughout the years I worked here. She said she didn't want to apply for the job initially, but when she heard that *I* was applying, she thought she might as well try it for herself and see if it could lead her toward a new career path. As a friend, you would think I would be happy for her. You would think that when someone you've known for many years and have developed a good friendship with goes after something she wants, she would deserve my blessings and well wishes, so that's what I gave her.

"This is great! I'm glad you decided to apply for the position," I told her.

We looked at each other and both remained in silence.

There were feelings inside of me that are hard to describe. The friendship between Cindy and me had changed over the years that we worked together in the hospital. She and I both had strong personalities, and there were times in the past when our personalities clashed. I was not happy about the way she used her condescending voice when she spoke to me, but once I got to know her better, it turned out that's just how she is, and it was really my own interpretation of the message she was trying to convey. When she got married back in 2011, I was invited to her bachelorette party, engagement party, and wedding.

One day I walked into work and my left eye was bothering me. It felt painful when I was driving, and by the time I arrived I could barely open my eyes. Cindy saw me and asked what happened, and I told her that as I was putting my contacts in that morning, I must have caused a little abrasion on my eye. Cindy walked me to the clinic and sat with me as I waited for a doctor to see me. Cindy had always been a good friend to me, and the feeling was mutual. We hung out quite often and had a good laugh here and there. But when I found out she decided to apply for that administrative management position I was going after, I felt betrayed. Had I not told her that I was applying, maybe she wouldn't have, either. That was not the only reason I felt this way. With our new executive director, Charles, whom she had known before, there was a shared ethnicity, shared language, and a shared cultural background; I knew I did not stand a chance in getting this position. All of my inner critic's voices and self-doubt tumbled like rocks landing on the friendship bond we had created.

With this kind of mindset, I walked into the interview with an attitude of "I need to win this" and "I need to impress them." I was nervous but tried to look and sound like I knew what I was doing. The truth is that the more I thought I could do this, the less it felt like this position would be mine. I was trying too hard, and when you have to try too hard at something, chances are you are not being your true self, and people will spot that.

A few days later, I was called into the executive director's office. Charles sat me down and told me what a great employee I was, and how he valued the work I had done throughout the years at the hospital. At the end of the conversation, he said the position had been offered to my friend Cindy. In that moment I was disappointed but I was afraid to show my emotions in front of him. I felt humiliated, so instead, I thanked him for his time. Charles asked for my continued support for the new management in the office and then he pulled the friendship card on me, saying, "You and Cindy are really good friends and I hope this new change doesn't stop you from supporting her."

What was I supposed to say—"You're wrong. I don't want to celebrate her success with her"?

Deep inside I felt jealous, disappointed, betrayed by the way I was treated, and angry. And instead of saying how I really felt, I kept all of these emotions inside. I smiled, agreed to give my full support to the new management team, and pretended to be fully understanding and appreciative of the outcome.

A few months later, after Cindy stepped into the new management role, the immediate supervising director, Melody, submitted her resignation letter. Melody's resignation was sudden and Cindy had just started her new position and was now forced to take on additional responsibilities with no prior experience in leading a team. In some ways, I was glad this wasn't me—that I wouldn't have to take on those extra responsibilities. Strangely, I also felt it was karma; this is what you get when you betray someone. With all these bottled up feelings and emotions toward Cindy, I decided to distance myself from her. There were many things I was having at that point that I didn't feel before in our friendship. There were decisions that were made by her that were completely out of impulse. I knew she was struggling to manage everything while balancing her marriage. She must have felt the change between us, so one day, she asked me to have dinner with her.

We sat down and talked.

She began by saying that she and some of her other friends at work had noticed changes in my relationship with her. She wanted to speak to me about her accepting the position, and wanted to make sure that I was OK with it.

"Of course! I'm happy for you." I told her. What else could I say?

The longer I stayed at my current position, the less happy and fulfilled I felt. Every day felt the same, both at work and at home. Every problem seemed so repetitive, and there were no obvious solutions for making things better. I felt drained coming home from work, so I began looking for balance elsewhere.

The universe works in mysterious ways. Just when we think all hope is gone, it sends us a different message. It was around this time that I began to dive even deeper into discovering my own inner world. I became curious about my own purpose and my own existence. Personal development opportunities started to present themselves to me, and I was able to engage with more people and experience conversations that had deeper meaning. I met friends online whom I would engage in meaningful, thought-provoking conversations with. We exchanged our ideas through blogs, email, and texts.

I also began to analyze and re-examine my life experiences. In particular, the loss of what I could have been—a normal person—was extremely painful to ponder. It was so painful and hopeless that it triggered something inside of me that compelled me to look for something deeper—deeper than what I could see on the surface. More profound than what I experienced in the physical world. Along this journey, the betrayal of friendships and rejection on my quest for love brought me to turning point.

Through the years of living in self-doubt, hopelessness, resentment, guilt, hurt, and disappointment, there comes a point of no return. You can either continue to live as you have been, or you can start living. For me, this was a time when I said to myself, "OK, enough is enough. We need to go."

But where? I wasn't sure.

I started this journey by searching for my purpose in the outer world.

"I would like to have killer abs with a six pack." I said to my friends at work and they laughed.

155

Chapter

Sixteen

"You gain strength, courage and confidence by every experience in which you really stop to look fear in the face. You are able to say to yourself, 'I have lived through this horror. I can take the next thing that comes along.' You must do the thing you think you cannot do."

— Eleanor Roosevelt, *You Learn by Living: Eleven Keys for a More Fulfilling Life*

I gained a significant amount of weight in the 10 years since I started working. I was covering many shifts where my job involved a lot of sitting and not much in the way of moving around. The workplace was stressful and demanding. On the days

I was at work, I would sit down immediately after eating. I worked late shifts and the timing of my meals fluctuated quite a bit, and I would often snack after I getting home late at night. During the week I didn't have any physical activity. I couldn't. By the time I was in my late 30s, I was already using two crutches to walk because of the pressure I had been putting on my back throughout the years.

I went to see a physical therapist once, after I started working in the retail pharmacy sector and could finally afford to pay for it with the insurance coverage the position brought. After assessing me, the physical therapist told me that, due to my body alignment, weight, and the way I had been walking all these years, the only way to permanently fix my problem was by having surgical intervention again. Did I want that?

Next, I consulted with an orthopedic surgeon. "Of course, we can surgically realign everything, and you can start from the beginning. But given that you are functional right now and there's really nothing wrong with you that would immediately damage your health, would you want to go through all that?"

I came home and gave it some thought. I was able to walk with my arm crutches, which really helped to ease the pressure on my back. I had a mortgage on my house, and I needed to work. Remembering the last time I had surgery and given the side effects I endured and the recovery time away from work, I wasn't sure I wanted to go through that whole process again. Mentally, physically, and emotionally,

I couldn't afford to go back to feeling the pain and experiencing the arduous rehabilitation process. I had no choice but to say "No, I don't want that."

I decided against surgery; my back pain was tolerable, even though my body was out of alignment, I was functional and could move around, so I told myself I'd just have to deal with it until I'm no longer able to do so.

This decision not to have medical intervention was not without consequences. I noticed as I got older that I tired more easily. I also wasn't sleeping well at night, probably from the stress at work. I felt I was being targeted at work by management because of things I had said in the past. I disagreed when I felt it was warranted, and had an opinion about the many new rules being implemented. I felt I was being retaliated against.

As I began reflecting on my personal development, I woke up one day and felt an urgent need for change. I wasn't sure what that change would be, but I knew I needed one.

I went out that day and drove myself to a tattoo parlor a friend had told me about. I went in with cash in my hand and walked up to the counter. The tall, thin latino man behind the counter had arms covered in tattoos.

"Can I help you?" he asked.

"I would like to get a tattoo," I said.

He looked at me as I stood in front of him. A tiny little woman with two arm crutches.

"Sure," he said. "What kind of tattoo?"

"I got this temporary henna tattoo in Vegas a few weeks ago," I replied, pointing at my arm. "Can you elaborate on this design?"

He took a look at the design on my left bicep—a butterfly with heart shaped antennae and wings that evoked a tribal style.

"Sure! I can do that," he said.

"Great! Let's do this!" I replied.

I spent just over three hours in the chair that day getting the first tattoo of my life. I knew I wanted a tattoo for years, to commemorate my 30th birthday. I didn't know when I'd get it, exactly, or *why*. There was a part of me that always wanted one, but I never had the courage to step into a tattoo shop and actually get one.

A few months earlier, I had met Jesse, a litigation attorney on Match.com, and we started dating after knowing each other just a few weeks. He had just picked me up for our second date and I was sitting in the passenger seat of his car as he drove. In my mind, I thought this was going to be great. I had made it to our second date and this was a sign that he wanted to see me again. But it was in that moment— just as I was just thinking that thought, that I heard him say, "I don't want you to get this wrong, but I really like you as a friend and nothing more."

There I was, listening to him tell me the same thing I had heard over and over and over, from so many different people: "I really like you, but let's just be friends."

As disappointed as I was, we ended up having a good conversation over dinner. We talked and I shared the idea of always wanting to get a tattoo. "Why haven't you?" he asked. I didn't know what to say. And I could think of was, "Yeah, why haven't I?"

We continued to see each other and hung out a couple of times after that night. It was fun and exciting to have someone on the other side of the phone responding to me; flirting and making sexual jokes and wanting to invite me over after turning him on with dirty text messages. But that wasn't enough for me, especially when he reminded me that we were just friends and that he needed to see sparks from his partner in order to move it forward. One day, I went out and bought a packet of sparklers. I invited him to a museum gallery and, when we sat down, I gave it to him.

I was hoping this would have been different and that he would have seen me for who I *was* and not how I *looked*. I was hoping that this time, it would work out and that for the first time in my life, there would be this one guy who didn't mind my appearance, and that I could win him with my personality. I was hoping that he would change his mind about me. I was hoping that I would finally have that normal life I always wanted. I dreamed that on a cold winter's day, I would be sitting on the patio outside, and on the other chair, there would be a man's blue sweater hanging over the back. In my fantasy, I am sitting there awaiting his return, with two cups of hot chocolate to warm our hands. This was my dream.

But love doesn't work that way. Love is not something you hope for, but rather, love is just love. You just love that person wholeheartedly. And every one of us is capable of such love. Love without conditions, without expectations, without hoping that the other person will change the way they feel about you or the way they see you. You just love them for who they are, no matter how they feel about you. Love is not something you can hope to have; you just have it. This type of love comes from within you.

It was clear to me that I was on a different path than he was. Looking back, I wondered what I was supposed to learn from this. What message was I supposed to take away from this encounter? Sitting in that chair at the tattoo shop that day, it finally occurred to me that the night when he asked me why I hadn't got that tattoo I always wanted, he provoked something else that was inside of me. And here I was sitting in a tattoo parlor shop getting this tattoo I have been wanting.

There are many things in our lives we know we want for ourselves, be it family, money, or a life full of happiness and prosperity. We *want* them, but wanting does not necessarily translate into action.

I knew I wanted a tattoo, so why hadn't I gotten one? One might argue that it was because tattoos hurt, they cost money, and maybe because they don't look professional. But when we want something and we've lived with that desire for many years, why is it that we fail to take action? Maybe it's not a good time, and maybe there will *never* be a good time to move toward achieving your goals. Maybe some disaster will strike tomorrow and we'll just end up dying along with our desires.

"I'd rather live a life full of 'oh well' than 'what if'."

Although it took me years to realize this, the day I sat in that chair getting my tattoo marked a new beginning. From that day on, I began a journey of self-discovery. I began to see my own light breaking through the gloomy sky. It was as if I had been sitting in a dark room for a long time and someone walked in and turned the lights on for me. All of a sudden, I could see things differently. It was a strange feeling at first. I started to be very curious about all the beliefs I had about myself. I read books on self-development, I listened to spiritual teachers on conscious awareness, I spoke with like-minded people, and I attended seminars in the pursuit of truth and wisdom. I was in the same room this whole time, but with the light switched on, I could see the door to lead me out.

When Jesse and I stopped communicating, I had just turned 39, and that was the year I finally got my tattoo.

It was also the year my sister, Emily, was getting married. I came home that day with the tattoo on my left arm. I went through the garage door and saw my mom sitting in the living room. I went up to her and told her that I got a tattoo. She looked at me and didn't say a word. Later that day, my sister called after seeing a post on my Facebook wall. The first thing she said to my mom was, "How could you let her get a tattoo?"

"What did you expect me to do?" Mom asked. "She's almost 40, she's free to do whatever she wants to do."

"Well, you are *not* coming to my wedding with that tattoo," Emily insisted. "You better cover it for my wedding."

So, I did. Besides getting the tattoo, I also dyed my hair red. Emily was furious but also concerned. "Are you going through a midlife crisis?" she asked.

Well, I probably wouldn't call it a midlife crisis, but I was definitely going through some changes.

Soon after getting the tattoo, I started looking into doing something more for myself. That feeling of "I am more than just my body" lead to a desire of wanting to be good to myself.

I bought a black dress to wear to my sister's wedding. It was a size two—my normal size—but parts of my body felt constricted when I put it on. I used to wear size xs clothing, but suddenly I noticed I had gone up two sizes. It was a sign for me to change. But how? I was dependent on two crutches to walk and had a pair of crooked legs, so how do I even begin to lose weight?

It's amazing how much you can do when you become curious about your capabilities. I went online and started to research "handicapped exercises," "people with disability and exercises," and "losing weight and exercise." You name it, I searched for them all. I was *determined*.

What worked really well for me was my healthcare background. With my knowledge as a pharmacist, I knew how to calculate my own caloric intake and determine how much I would need to start losing weight. I sat down and mapped out my total calorie count needed to survive and how much I would need to eliminate in order to start losing weight. I downloaded an app on my phone to track my own consumption habits. I began reading labels on products I picked up from the grocery store. Like many people on the path to weight loss, I started to count calories. This meal would be 300 calories, that meal would be 400 calories, and I'd keep track of everything on my plate. I kept a food journal and tracked my weight.

This method was effective, but not entirely healthy. Initially, I lost five pounds just by keeping an eye on what I ate. Later this turned into shaming myself to avoid eating too much. There were days where I only eat half of a bagel so I didn't have to feel guilty about consuming carbohydrates. I stopped putting sugar in my coffee and began tracking my daily sugar intake. I was on a roll and I had a mission to lose weight.

My initial intention was simply to do what was good for myself. What it meant for me was going back to my size xs clothing. It started when I was in my car one day, wearing a white t-shirt and a pair of jeans. As I got out of my car, I noticed a black mark around my stomach. For a long time, I couldn't figure out what it was. But as I started to observe more closely, I realized my stomach had gotten so big that it was rubbing against the steering wheel each time I made a turn. It was shocking that I had allowed myself to put on this much weight. That feeling of "not good enough" and shame showed up, but this time I decided to do something about it.

Eventually, I came to a point where my weight was not dropping; I had reached a plateau. "This is not happening!" I told myself. I was already eating a lot less than usual and the weight just wasn't moving. This sparked my curiosity to discover what steps I needed to take, and it turned out that the only way to get over this weight loss plateau was to start exercising.

"Well, great! Now what?" I said to myself. "I can't run, and I have never been to a gym. I don't know how to exercise."

I was beginning to see a pattern in myself. The minute I came across a challenge, I immediately hit the replay on that voice in my head. All the "I can't," "I don't," "I wouldn't," and "I shouldn't" began to take control over my behavior. I kept myself small, hiding behind the curtains. I stopped believing in myself. The more I looked into it, the more aware I became of my own actions.

The next day I bought myself a balance ball and a yoga mat.

"Well, I know I can't run; but I can probably sit on the balance ball and work on my problem areas. Since my stomach is my problem area, maybe if I start working on my belly, it would help to get over this hump."

This worked for a few weeks until I hit a plateau again. This time, I really took a step up to play the game. I decided to join a gym and take yoga classes for the first time in my life. I wasn't sure what I could do as a person with a disability, walking into a gym with two arm crutches, but I knew I had to do something. Just like the day I got out of surgery, sitting on the hospital bed holding my legs and wishing things would be different, I wanted to do something to change my situation. There was a feeling that arose within me that pushed me to do something different in my life. I felt I was more ready than ever to get up and go. And I hired myself a personal trainer. I needed someone to help me reach my goal. I needed help!

I had a goal in mind: hiking the Inca Trail to Machu Picchu the following year. I wanted to experience what it was like to be a "normal" person. I wanted to prove to myself that I could do this.

I began by taking walks in a nearby park. The first time, I walked the running track, it was challenging. People were watching. I used my two arm crutches as walking poles, and I walked around the track. Every day I got up before dawn to join others in the park for a walk. Week in and week out, I slowly went from 0.8 miles to three miles over the course of six months. There were days my arms were sore and my wrist hurts, but I took some ibuprofen and kept walking. My personal trainer, Rob, was also very supportive. He trained me every week and designed a fitness program tailored to my ability. We sat down, came up with a plan of how to work around my limitations and he modified exercises to accommodate my height and my range of motion. Instead of having me run on a treadmill when we worked on cardio exercises, he would have me walk or slam balls and pull ropes. Before I realized it, I was walking a 5K marathon. I also started to hike in the mountains and hills in my neighborhood. Every weekend, I'd wake up and pack my bag and hike up to the mountain to prepare for my Machu Picchu trip.

Next, I booked myself a ticket to travel on a solo adventure to Peru in September of 2016.

Chapter

Seventeen

"I define connection as the energy that exists between people when they feel seen, heard, and valued; when they can give and receive without judgment; and when they derive sustenance and strength from the relationship."

— Brené Brown, *The Gifts of Imperfection*

During the transition to a new management team at the hospital, staff was asked to bring suggestions and ideas to discuss, and I had a lot of ideas for how to improve workflow and team dynamics. When I brought the ideas up at meetings, they were turned down. I also noticed that the overall team engagement had decreased significantly compared to when I first started with the company.

There were more sick calls at work, which created an additional workload for me and other staff. I felt frustrated and stressed just thinking about going to work.

This is how the mysterious universe works when we feel stuck or need a sign to help us determine our direction in life. It is in those moments when we feel hopeless and need some guidance to move forward that the universe begins sending us signals. There may be people who show up in our lives unexpectedly—people who prompt us to say to ourselves, "I must have known this person in a previous life." They come bearing a purpose: to plant a seed of wisdom appropriate for the current stage in our lives. Some call these people their soulmates; others refer to them as their best friends. Whatever name we decide to give them, they are here for one thing and one thing only: to help open our eyes and widen our horizons so we can become who we were always meant to be. They are here to awaken the parts of ourselves that have been asleep for the longest time.

On my own path of awakening, these people have suddenly appeared in my life, sparking a sense of connectedness and togetherness. People who share my thoughts and beliefs about what the world is and what it should be. These people speak to my soul and I feel safe whenever they are near. I am fortunate to have met many of them. Each one of them brings up topics and ideas that challenge my own thoughts, teaching me valuable life lessons. Among all my friends, there is one who stands out as the dearest to me. This is someone who sat with me on a day when I was having a complete meltdown and begging the universe for a sign.

I met Jack when I was 41, while I was gearing up for my Machu Picchu hike. I walked into a gym and Jack was one of the personal trainers who worked there. We met and talked every time I bumped into him at the gym. We had a lot in common; we both liked the '80s rock music and books on spirituality, and we both wanted to do something greater for the benefit of humankind. I wanted to open up a charity school to benefit the children of refugees, and he wanted to use his musical talent to inspire people affected by the crisis in the Middle East.

One summer's day, Jack sat with me under a tall, beautiful tulip tree. As I sat there asking, "Why? Why? Why me? Why do things always happen to me? Why am I here?" Jack took out his phone, pulled up all the quotes he had collected throughout the years that he turned to for inspiration, and he read them one by one with me. "Look: No one has the answers to 'Why?' and there are always going to be some very tough days," he said. "Just keep doing what you are doing, and maybe someday, we'll find out the answers."

I looked into his eyes and felt a sense of relief. It was the sense that someone understood what I was saying and knew how I felt, having experienced the same battles as I had. With the common beliefs, values, and understandings about life that Jack and I shared, we developed a strong bond over the next few years. We enjoyed going to concerts and movies together, and hanging out late at night to celebrate each other's birthday. And since we were both interested in spirituality, we even decided to go on a retreat together.

Isn't this how love is supposed to be?

This one person sitting in front of you and you get along so well, you make each other laugh, respect each other. You can call them five times a day and they will not think you're crazy. You can tell them anything. Well, of course, it is easy when you are just friends, because there is no pressure and no sex. The easier things are between you, the easier it seems to take that next step. However, it is frustrating when you cannot just do it.

But as it turned out, this was also the worst place to be. At one point in our journey together, he wanted to tell me about all the other people he wanted to date, and all I could do was be a good sport and give him the best advice I could, outside of "forget about them and date me. Can't you see?" At times, it felt like dating, only without the physical intimacy: going out to dinner, the movies, spending quality time together. We were bonding, and the connection grew stronger over time.

There is the old "don't rock the boat" rule. You value your friendship, and taking the next step might destroy it. Even if you are not afraid of destroying the friendship by taking the next step, you still hold back because you know the other person sees you as just a good friend. When you are sad, he understands you. When he is waking up in a state of panic, you are there to sit with him in the dark.

But all your feelings are left to burn inside, hidden away, while your friend clearly has no interest in taking this friendship to another level. If you are very close, every time your friend is hurt or frustrated in love, they might come to you for solace and comfort. You have to sit there watching different people hurt them and take them for granted, knowing you would give them the world and treat them right if you were together. However, all you can do is be there for them when they are hurt before they move on to the next person that isn't you.

It's simple, if not easy, to deal with feelings for someone you don't know well. You suffer, you cry, you write poems, and then eventually you move on. But when it's someone you are friends with, it gets trickier. You want them to stay in your life. You can't always avoid seeing them while you nurse your broken heart. And because you know them so well, your feelings for them have deeper roots and take longer to die down.

Do I continue seeing him and respond to his calls and texts? Do I jeopardize our friendship by telling him how I truly feel? Do I continue on with the friendship in the hope that my feelings will eventually go away?

When I found out I had deep feelings for him but he was dating someone else again, I was haunted by a series of thoughts:

"What if this is she ends up being The Woman?"

"They'll get married, buy a house, and have kids—everything that I long for with him, but I'll never have because we are simply friends."

"Can I fault him for telling me this? Of course, not. We're friends."

The voice in my head showed up every time he brought up his relationship status and dating life. And as much as I would have liked to sit there and give him advice about how to win a woman's heart, my jealousy overruled me.

"Someday, I want to introduce my wife to you." Jack said. "I bet my kids would like playing with you."

Those were the days I deepened my meditation practice and took deep breaths to cool my mind. These strategies helped me realize that the disappointment couldn't be ignored, but that just like all emotions, they would pass like waves on the shore. I kept reminding myself that we are all impermanent beings and we cannot expect our relationships or those in our lives to remain static.

"Don't play the blame game." I told myself. "You chose to stay as his friend."

But true friends do not wish to harm each other in any way. There were times I caught myself focusing on the rejection and the sense of injustice I felt because my friend did not reciprocate my feelings, but I never doubted Jack's respect for me nor his goodwill towards all sentient beings. He was honest and could not lie just to spare my feelings or curb my disappointment. I didn't blame him for being honest, caring, and wanting to offer his lifelong friendship.

There were days I saw him that I felt compelled to accept that offer to simply be his lifelong friend.

After I revealed my feelings and chose to stay within the friendship zone, I continued to find myself haunted by my own desire for more. It was time for me to do something differently. I took a chance. I picked a distance. I drew my line and expressed my wish to have space from him. I did not want to see him. I chose not to be around him.

I don't regret this choice and don't blame myself nor him for the way things worked out. I knew my decision hurt him as much as it hurt me, but I believe true friends eventually understand what is best for the other person to heal their wounds, and that they will forgive the pain you both have experienced.

No more hanging around at the end of the day to chitchat. No email, notes, or phone calls. Yes, it was painful, and it would take time. Sooner or later, what started out as "I am so happy I don't have to see my friend while feeling hurt with a knot in my heart" will turn into an appreciation for nature, sharing laughter with friends, and enjoying a beautiful sunset. Most importantly, I needed time to exercise the same compassion and tenderness to myself that I had so willingly offered to others.

A lot of the pain I felt walking away from this platonic love came from feeling that our energies and time were wasted and meaningless. My feelings for my friend were powerful, important, and real, and to think of him as something that I just needed to "get over" felt wrong on a visceral level. So instead, I thought of other things I could do with those feelings.

Having had this friendship was the most amazing thing that happened to me over a time span of four years. I learned things I would never imagined I'd learn; I had gone to places I had never been before, because I had been alone. This friendship meant the world to me.

In 2018, when Jack and I took a walk behind the building where he works, he told me about his nephew, who was considering hiring a "life coach" to help him overcome his anxiety problem. As Jack described this process of looking for a life coach, something awakened in me. I was curious about what a life coach was and did. I never heard of such a profession, but it felt like a breakthrough in that moment—like a blade of grass doggedly pushing through the cracks in a concrete sidewalk. I went home that day, sat down in front of my computer, and typed "life coach" into Google.

Those words created a vibration within me. I started reading up on what a life coach is and what makes them unique. What I discovered was that life coaching is a profession that is profoundly different from consulting, mentoring, therapy, advice-giving, or counseling. It is a designed alliance between the coach and the client, where the process addresses specific personal projects, business successes, general conditions and transitions in personal life, relationships, or professions by examining what is going on right now, discovering what obstacles or challenges might stand in the way, and choosing a course of action to make life be what the client wants it to be.

Every day we make choices to do or *not* do certain things. These choices can range from profound to trivial. Each one has an effect that makes our lives more fulfilling or less fulfilling, more balanced or less balanced, our process of living more effective or less effective. Being a life coach means being able to help others learn to make those choices that create an effective, balanced, and fulfilling life.

I took a long look back at my own life: the agony of pain and suffering, the experiences of hopelessness, the fear and panic felt in the middle of the night that shook me off my bed. I had been forced to make choices in every stage of my life, and experienced challenges and discouragement along the way. Those "Why? Why? Why?" questions suddenly became clear to me: in every moment of our lives, we have choices to make.

I could have chosen to live my life in regret, resentment, disappointment, or struggle. Or I could choose to live my life with calm, clarity, confidence, love, and fulfilment. To say I am all butterflies, happiness, and self-love 100 percent of the time would be dishonest and an overstatement, but now, compassion rules. I became passionate about helping people going through major life transitions become, in a way, the master of their own minds, bodies, and feelings, because this is where self-acceptance comes in. I didn't become passionate about coaching overnight; it was through the years of struggles and through all the ups and downs that I discovered what makes my life worth living.

No matter how desperate you are in this moment, no matter how much pain you are holding in your heart, no matter how much fear you have that's haunting you at night, it is possible to make a choice; a conscious choice. It is possible to turn on that torch—the fire within your heart—and make a comeback. It is possible to let go of your painful memories and embrace them with love and tender care. And it is absolutely possible to begin leading yourself out of the misery and tragedy life's circumstances put you in. It is possible because there is a light within every one of us.

Jack and I chose to go our separate ways during the early development stage of this part of my life's journey. I am not sure we will ever become friends again, but I never doubted that the friendship we had devoted ourselves to over the years had been nothing but the best it could be.. I always liked the analogy of taking a bus ride: Somewhere along this journey of life, we both got on the same bus. We sat next to each other for a very long time and shared memories together on this path. But the bus came to a stop and I made the decision to get off. I have reasons to believe that, even as we have decided to respect each other's choice, we are still walking each other home.

There are times I catch myself asking, "Will I ever forget him or love him any less because he didn't love me back?" The answer has always been clear to me. To be able to love someone unconditionally, in the words of psychotherapist and spiritual teacher Anthony de Mello, is like listening to the music in a symphony without attachment.

He is the music. Jack reminded me of the happy notes that a stranger had played on my guitar many years ago at the airport on my way to America. And regardless of where we are, Jack will always be the music to my ears and he will always have a place in my heart.

Chapter

Eighteen

"Life isn't to be lived just waiting. No one is coming to save you. No one is riding in like a knight in shining armor. It's time to save yourself."

— Michelle Kuei

For many years, I was afraid to show people my most vulnerable self. I was afraid to be seen and known. In order to be seen and known, I would need to tell you about my story. I hardly ever talk about myself and share my past to anyone. It wasn't until recent years, when I started my journey toward self-mastery, that I began to see the value of authenticity. Authenticity means being honest with ourselves and being honest with everyone else.

My different appearance became a label I put onto

myself. My unique appearance was a label I put onto myself. Yes, I looked different, but I still wanted to be loved just as much as the next person. I wanted to be seen and heard, and to have a "normal" life where I could fit in with the crowd. But no matter where I go or who I am with, I always stand out. Embracing this instead of resisting it was a big step forward.

Throughout my journey I've come to realize that we set standards for ourselves that are often too high because society expects us to be perfect. We are brought up with beliefs that are deeply rooted and passed down through generations. Standards that dictate how a woman should look and what we should wear; standards that perpetuate the myth that "men don't cry,"and other harmful ideas that shape our understanding about how the world should be. We forget that everybody has flaws, including the people we perceive as perfect. But who decides what perfection is? Who sets the standards we feel we need to live up to?

Flaws are what make us human. Everybody makes mistakes. That is the only way we can learn and grow. Accepting our flaws and forgiving ourselves for our mistakes and reconciling those conflicting parts of ourselves is crucial to our health and happiness, and generally, to achieving our greatest potential as humans. Judging ourselves harshly constricts and lowers the energy in our bodies, and also plays a role in virtually all manner of physical, mental, and emotional health problems. The pressure to be a certain way or look a certain way to gain acceptance is everywhere.

But it is only when we decide to accept and love ourselves that all kinds of good things start to happen.

There is a phrase we use and hear often: "Taking up space." It means that you value yourself and recognize your own existence. You have every right to occupy the space you're in. When your rights are being violated or compromised, you take up space and speak up. It's a call to rise up and change how you see yourself. *Be* the change.

It also means that when you enter a room, you make sure you are not being pushed into a corner of that room. Show up with your kindness, with your generosity, and with your vulnerability by sharing your story with people. Be genuine. Be authentic. When you put yourself out there, you will get feedback; some may be positive, and some negative. Some people may like you and others may not. You can't make everyone happy, and that's OK! Because if you're living life in accordance with your own values, then you're going to have to know when to ignore other people, and understand that making yourself happy doesn't always mean making everyone around you happy. You can't change how others see the world, but you can change how *you* see the world.

There are many things I have learned on my journey about taking up space in the world. The world needs each and every one of us to embrace our special gifts and to step into our light. Whether you believe it or not, you do have special gifts and you were created to make a difference in this lifetime. There will always be that one person who needs the smile you didn't wear this morning when you showed up to work. There will always be someone who needs that book you did not write or that song you never composed. And there will always be someone who needs to hear the story you never told.

Two days prior to my Inca Trail hike, I experienced high altitude syndrome. Being in a foreign country and not speaking the local language, I found myself dragging my feet to the hotel lobby where I asked the concierge to contact a doctor for me. The following day, I checked myself into an urgent care clinic in Peru where I received medical attention. Forty-eight hours later, I was standing in front of the Inca Trailhead, eager to take on a big journey of my lifetime.

Perseverance is the ability to keep doing something in spite of obstacles. People who persevere show steadfastness in doing something despite how hard it is or how long it takes to reach that goal. Perseverance calls for consistency. Consistently in moving toward your goals. It is the act of becoming a master at your own craft and it takes a lot of hard work. You will experience messy frustrations, and your motivation will come and go, but you can only improve when you commit to constant practice. You will make countless mistakes during the process. You may lose and gain friends on this journey. It is a mixture of passion, self-discipline, and self-acceptance that keeps us moving forward in spite of the obstacles.

The world needs dreamers and doers. The world needs you to dance because the world wants to dance with you. And the world needs people who spend their time doing things they believe in. But most importantly, the world needs your light.

Perhaps you live life just waiting in anticipation for that next vacation, that next big event, or a quick fix in the hope that it will bring some sort of peace, comfort, or freedom from your daily stress, exhaustion, burn-out, or misery. You may be on edge, unhappy, ungrateful, and unfulfilled.

Some of us experience tragedies as a rude wakeup call, but not everyone has to go through this. Not everyone needs to wait for a disaster to happen to really begin living. Nor is life to be lived just waiting for that thing to put you back into a state of happiness and flow. Because when you return from vacay, the issues haven't gone anywhere, the credit card debt is still stacked up, the relationship is still in pieces, and you have to return to that job you hate.

The truth is, no one is coming to save you. No one is riding in like a knight in shining armor. It is time to save yourself. It is a choice. And it is time to own up to your happiness. It is time to switch on the light on and step into your true power!

Throughout my post-accident life journey, I took my time in getting to this place. I spent years in anger, steeped in feelings of loss, shame, and struggle. I was in the process of discovering who I am and what I was meant to do in this lifetime. I thought I would have a normal body shape, an average height, a good education, a great career that pays the bills, and perhaps I would have been married by now with children. I would have been living in a house filled with laughter. My husband and I would be loving and respectful of each other. We would have a dog or a cat, and would have saved up money to allow us to travel. Everything that everyone dreams of and everything that is considered "normal" under normal circumstances. But my life didn't happen under "normal" circumstances; instead it took a big turn when I was just 11 years old.

Life isn't about becoming. It's not about becoming successful or becoming more powerful or stronger. Instead, life is about "un-becoming." It is about un-becoming the person you thought you were. Un-becoming the angry and frustrated person that keeps you from reaching forgiveness. It is about un-becoming the person hindered by false ideas about yourself that keep you from starting a new project or living a new life. It is certainly about un-becoming what others expect you to be. Perhaps our stories shouldn't be compared to those of a caterpillar becoming a butterfly, but rather how a butterfly is *un-becoming* what it isn't.

To be brave and step into the true essence of yourself doesn't take much. Even just a little bit is good enough. Through my journey, the most profound thing I have learned is that there is no escape from my own fears. Fear of not being liked. Fear of not being good enough. Fear of being different from everyone else. Fear is the enemy we will battle till death.

The good news is that just as fear is inescapable, bravery is utterly attainable. Bravery requires endurance; it requires persistence and perseverance. It is that thing that keeps you going after you come to a stop at a metaphorical stop sign. Bravery is a choice, and the willingness to confront your agony, your pain, danger, uncertainty, or intimidations in life.

We experience change through adversity and challenges in order to rise to a higher functioning state. Many of our circumstances represent challenges to adapt, and pose significant challenges to the way we understand the world. There is value in every instance of pain and suffering. It is in those moments of low tide that we learn about truth and about ourselves, and it is in those roaring storms that we see the light of hope.

Stories like mine can be heartbreaking, but my story can also spark the joy within us. We all have stories and struggles that we dare not tell anyone when we meet them. There are people out there who genuinely care about us and are willing to share out struggles, but instead of opening up, we hide ourselves away from being seen or heard. We hide the struggles and stories that tell people *who we are*.

My stories and my struggles are no greater or bigger than yours. What is tragic to me can be the most insignificant chapter in another person's life. But we each have our challenges; not one challenge is bigger or smaller, because within every one of those challenges lies the opportunity to live a more meaningful life. First comes the pain, then comes the opportunity to rise up.

Behind every trauma there is an untold story. It is the untold story of adversity and resilience—the heroic, powerful, and perilous lifelong journey.

In your life as in mine, there are reasons why our journey unfold the way they do. For me, discovering what makes my life worth living and how to show up fully in life was the lesson I needed to learn. And no matter how desperate you are in this moment, no matter how much pain you are holding in your heart, no matter how much fear you have that's haunting you at night, it is possible to let go of painful memories and embrace them with tender love and care.

My story is one of courage, determination, and vulnerability. But more importantly, it is about having the confidence to face fear in everyday life. Everyone goes through difficult times, yet we still manage to wake up every morning and take that first deep breath and get on with the day.

At any given moment, you can choose how you want to move forward with your life. You can cry your heart out over all the things you have lost in life or you can sit and wait for all the miracles to find their way to you. You can take action or no action at all. Depending on your perceptions about your own circumstances, you can choose to live your life differently—or not. The value of getting rid of things that no longer serve us can be challenging, but it is the fundamental teaching behind reclaiming our power and finding clarity within our lives. Removing illusions and ignorance allows us to reveal what is real, true, and beautiful. What we need is to take a leap forward and abandon the fear that holds us back, and let go of not being good enough while also cultivating gratitude and appreciation for who we are.

There are methods we can use to identify what's holding us back, whether it's fear, limiting beliefs, or the unconscious mind. Then we can eliminate each obstacle to reach our goals. You are the only one who has the power to become your true self: invincible, fearless, and powerful.

Made in the USA
Columbia, SC
22 November 2019